The Enneagram Effect

A Self Discovery Roadmap, Master Effective Communication with 9 Personality types even in toxic relationships

Ryan Burton

ISBN 978-0-6486577-0-5

Table of Contents

Introduction 1
Chapter One: Definition And Understanding Of Enneagram 5
Chapter Two: The History Of Enneagram 9
Chapter Three: Where Enneagram Was Developed 13
Chapter Four: Why Choose Enneagram And What Are The Benefits You Can Get From It? 17
Chapter Five: The First Personality 22
Chapter Six: The Second Personality 27
Chapter Seven: The Third Personality 33
Chapter Eight: The Fourth Personality 39
Chapter Nine: The Fifth Personality 44
Chapter Ten: The Sixth Personality 49
Chapter Eleven: The Seventh Personality 54
Chapter Twelve: The Eighth Personality 59
Chapter Thirteen: The Ninth Personality 64
Chapter Fourteen: The Instinctual Variants Of Enneagram 69
Chapter Fifteen: The Enneagram And Social Relations 74
Chapter Sixteen: The Enneagram And Parenting 78
Chapter Seventeen: The Intelligence Of Enneagram 83
Chapter Eighteen: The Application Of Enneagram 90
Chapter Nineteen: The Wings Of The Enneagram Personalities ... 93
Chapter Twenty: The Neuroscience Of Enneagram 97
Conclusion 100
References 101

Introduction

Hi there! Have you ever heard of the term; "Enneagram?" If you have, then congratulations. Getting to know about it is the first step, but applying it is the second and bold step. If you haven't, then it's no big deal. As a matter of fact, I was once in that position too. There were times I would even find myself in places I didn't even know I was; in a state, I could never have imagined myself in, a situation where I didn't understand the people around me. Trust me; it's not a good place to be.

But thanks to Enneagram, I was able to move past every hurdle and obstacle that had sworn to make my life miserable. I was ready to go into a fantastic state of understanding myself. With the understanding of the nine personality traits, I have been able to interact, mingle, and understand anybody that crosses my path, no matter how complicated some people appear to be. That is what Enneagram teaches you. Don't be surprised, it's all real, and it is precisely what I'm going to show you in the course of this book.

Now, don't get it twisted, Enneagram is no joke, neither is it something hard to pull off as many people had painted it over the past few years. It is, in fact, one of the simplest types of personality trait that you can study within the shortest time. Enneagram would give you a sound understanding of who you are, what your personality is, and a comprehensive understanding of the people around you.

In the words of Williams Shakespeare, I quote;

"If you don't understand yourself, nobody will understand you."

Be that as it may, Enneagram is the study of the nine personalities of people that shows you exactly how the human mind works and how various people react in different situations. You also need to know that understanding people also helps you determine your personality. This is because there is a high probability that the people whom you intend studying might also be studying you in return. Thus, the need for a complete understanding of Enneagram.

As a beginner in this field, it is essential to know that the relationships you have in society helps determine who you are. What happens then if you don't know anything about the society you live in? Your relationship with people will not turn out well and most likely not stand the test of time. While Enneagram is primarily used for understanding other people, it also gives a hint of who you are. It is pertinent to know that life situations go beyond personal dealings. If you have some knowledge about the personality of the people around you then relating with them on a more genuine level will undoubtedly be very easy. In other words, equating and understanding the nine personalities of people are the fundamental goals of this book.

There have been many books on Enneagram, but none of them could have combined the basic understanding of the concept with the in-depth knowledge in such a way that the beginners of Enneagram won't find the idea too difficult to handle. This is why the language used in this book is conversational and straightforward. Enneagram is not a complex phenomenon; it is a natural attribute that everyone possesses. Learning about our own personality helps in different ways. We can all enjoy who we are and our personality traits even better once we discover ourselves.

This book will serve as a simple guide for everyone on the Enneagram. Regardless of whether you are an expert or new to the concept, this book is meant for you. As an expert, you must have been familiar with this concept before now. However, there are lots of various insights that this book will expose you to, that you might not have heard of before. This book is designed to broaden your horizon and make you see beyond your level of imagination. On the other hand, as a beginner, it would build you up from scratch till you become an expert of your own in Enneagram.

As you go through the book, prepare to delve into the origin of the Enneagram, and then read on to learn about the latest research. The necessity of this is that you would be able to understand why and how Enneagram came into being and therefore, be confident in applying the knowledge, in your everyday life. It is also very paramount to know that social relations and behaviors of people cannot be guessed or given a thumbnail rule, but the underlying or causal factors could be understood. In short, you will learn, in the simplest way, underlying factors that impact the way people react to you and of course, how to deal with them appropriately.

Have you ever spoken to someone, and the reaction was different from what you expected? Have you ever noticed how different people would react in different situations? Do you think these are all just serendipity of behaviors? Understanding these strange behaviors is the goal of this book.

This is a book that combines personalities and their instincts. Many people have been waiting for a book that have these combinations even though there had been lots of books written in the past to fit one or the other. Now, the good news we bring is this - you can now get both combinations in a single book – this book. The majority of books that have been written on the topic have focused on these two combinations had always been written on religious grounds and tenets.

In other words, the nine personalities and their instincts have only been discussed in the religious setting over the years, with less consideration for other relations. After all, you can't use one single occurrence, religion, to determine all other ones. Aside from this combination, the style of the nine personalities is dealt with to get every bit of how Enneagram could be seen. This is where instincts are explained in clear and straightforward terms. An overview of the personalities through the diagram is described. The diagram will explain each style and how they are related.

In this book, you will also learn the primary and subsidiary personality of people through the understanding of the neuroscience of Enneagram. While many psychologists believe that there are nine personalities of people, neuroscientists discussed that one could detect some play-in-group personalities. In other words, the personalities of people, according to the neuroscience of Enneagram, are made up of two different components: the primary and secondary personality traits. We will go through all of that will throughout this book.

Additionally, as a parent or potential parent, you will learn how to handle your children with an understanding of their personalities. Of course, not everyone is a parent. However, everyone has had to deal with situations where these lessons can be applied. There is no denying that parenting is a complicated thing to do; however, when you understand it from the angle of the people's personalities, it becomes easier. This book will provide you every bit of this understanding.

Many people wonder why and how Enneagram applies to them. This is because many books have focused primarily on other people: this is a different book. You will learn how to apply these personalities to not only you but other situations around you as well. You will be taken through a personality test. This test will be used to ascertain the personalities of the people around you, and that would be within the shortest possible time. Instead of following other methods that would waste your precious time and end up eating through your timeline, Enneagram would save you from time-wasting, it is fast, reliable, and perfect.

You can see this new skill (knowing the personality of people within the shortest time) as a detective trait in you. You now possess the power to see through people, to understand the emotions & personalities of people, and to make use of the nine personality traits to your advantage. One last thing you need to know before we start this journey together, do not misuse the knowledge you will gain from this book. Being selfless is of the essence when reading people's personality. When we help people become a better version of what they were yesterday by reading through their personality, then we are doing a good thing. But using those same powers to manipulate anyone is merely unacceptable.

It is important to remember that this book has been constructed to give you an introduction to what Enneagram is all about. This is why it is for everyone. Its ultimate goal is to familiarize you with the knowledge of the concept of Enneagram in the simplest way. While going about that dream job, have you ever wondered who will be conducting the interview? What they're like? What makes them tick? Well, the trick is in this book. Now, let's get to it, shall we?

Chapter One
Definition and Understanding of Enneagram

To begin with, the term Enneagram is a simple term which can be quite complicated in its understanding. However, with the help of this chapter, you will be able to create your definition on the concept. Being able to do so is essential in that it ensures that you understand the real meaning of Enneagram. The Enneagram can be defined as the study of human personalities, especially in their relationships or behaviors in a social setting. It is also a model for identification of who we actually are, and the nine personality types that are used in the analysis.

It is essential to know that because of how extensive the study is; it has different concepts aimed at different purposes but with a fundamental notion of "nine human personalities study." As a model, the Enneagram is understood to be a collection of interrelated personality types. Take for example, when you're around people, and you notice that some people are optimistic, happy and energetic, some are dull, or even in despair, some could be moving around aimlessly, while some remain quite still. Without knowing it, you have just conducted an enneagram study on those people.

As a typology of human personalities, Enneagram is referred to as the nine shades or sometimes called Enneatypes. This is indicated by a geometric figure known as enneagram points. It is the point where different personalities within a specified geometry meet with the reactions of different people at the same given scenario.

The growth of Enneagram has been tremendous and alarming at the spiritual and business levels as it had garnered momentum as regards these levels over the past few years. This is because they are the two significant social settings that deal with the co-existence of people for a relatively long time. The need to study Enneagram across the bounds of a specific geographical setting is pertinent. This is because even within two people, social relations can be established. Think about this, when you are in a conversation with someone, and suddenly their reaction dramatically changes - try to understand what caused this change.

In the long run, you will come to realize that everything boils down to your Enneagram. In other words, your personality and that of the other person's. It's little wonder why Enneagram is very important in our lives for a successful relationship with the people around us. These personalities are interwoven with yours, and they determine your relationships with people as well. In the line of business, Enneagram means the act of gaining more knowledge of how dynamic interpersonal thoughts affect diverse workers in their approaches to tasks at the workplaces. Interviewers use this Enneagram as a concept and a working mechanism in determining how the candidates will react to events surrounding them.

This will tell them the best candidates for their job. Instead of asking these workers about their job functions and responsibilities, Enneagram would focus more on the personalities of the workers as related to their line of duty. All of this is Enneagram at play. While in the spiritual setting, Enneagram is seen as what depicts a meaningful living and also an awareness of the state of living. Now the question we should ask ourselves is if this is all about Enneagram. This is how Enneagram operates spiritually in the real sense of the world. Be that as it may, we shouldn't forget that Enneagram is a broad concept with diverse settings and usage. Although they might seem to be an embodiment of these nine personality traits, they are also independent but interrelated. Furthermore, Enneagram is the best state or personalities believed to be true for all humans.

Additionally, the Enneagram is perceived as a personality system which combines nine different traits. Many accentuations have been made regarding the fact that humans have one of these personalities which consist of some subtypes as well. Well, you might wonder how these traits get to us; many people say we pick them up in childhood while other people say it is genetically related. Whatever your belief might be about these two assumptions, the fact that everyone behaves within specified traits in different ways remains true for every situation.

There are nine types of Enneagram generally. There are different attachments to these types, and they all have a placement within the symbol of the Enneagram. The nine personalities have different names, and they are as follows:

1. The Reformer,
2. The Helpers,
3. The Achievers,
4. The Individualist,
5. The Investigators,
6. The Loyalists,
7. The Enthusiasts,
8. The Challenger,
9. The Peacemakers.

In all the studies of Enneagram, one repeated and fascinating factor that has come up is that people within a given type of trait will be different from one another. The reason for this is yet to be ascertained, but it could be because humans are dynamic. In fact, everyone, including you, could be a challenger within a particular time and then change to an enthusiast some other times.

Many psychologists believe that every change in human traits premises on the state of mental health. Further opinions are still subject to researchers though. Healthiness or unhealthiness state is defined as what a particularly given quality finds pleasurable and natural to them against what they see and do as otherwise. The focus of this chapter is not to provide in-depth information about the personalities; it will be dealt with in the chapters to follow.

However, it is to open your mind and introduce you to the concept of Enneagram. That way, you will be able to understand the following chapters as you read them. There are different levels in the personalities' types which contribute to their healthiness as well. In order to explain Enneagram in total, there are separate wings created for them. These wings will be adequately discussed later in this book.

However, what they explain is the fact that many people have combinations of Enneagram personalities. Even though the nine personalities are true to humans, there are more combinations to these personalities than the existence of their singular presence. This makes postulation of rules that capture their behavior a mirage and vague.

It is pertinent to note that there are different names given to these personalities. This could be because they have different teachings, context, and usage of the information. Whatever angle enneagram studies might take in the future, one fact remains that it is a nine-personality study and a model to understanding the ways, actions, and reactions that occur in social relationships.

In conclusion, Enneagram encapsulates the system of the nine human personalities that determine the trait which signals why people react and act in the way they do. The people that developed it might have not even imagined it could be real Enneagram. This is because many people have altered the probability of having the Enneagram in its holistic nature. , but its reality is shown even in these non believers. This is the power of Enneagram.

Trust me -nothing is stopping you from becoming a better version of yourself - besides yourself. You are your own biggest rival and enemy towards achieving this fantastic trait. If only you can look past your weaknesses and emotions, understanding people's personalities would be at your fingertips. That way, you would be able to thrive in your workplace, relationships, and other social outings. The next chapter focuses on how Enneagram began as a concept, idea, and term. You don't want to miss it.

Chapter Two
The History of Enneagram

As the old saying goes, everything that has a beginning has an end - and vise versa. Every process has a starting point, and every piece of history is felt in the future. This same situation extends to Enneagram. To fully understand what the term Enneagram means, we would have to go deep into its historical background and development. How did Enneagram begin? What led to its development? How was the idea of Enneagram conceived? There is only one way to find out as this is what this chapter will delve into.

The word Enneagram is from two Greek words, ennea, which means "nine" and gramma meaning "written." The origin of Enneagram has been a notable controversy among scholars. The need arose because many people have found the personalities identified as being true to form even in their personal experiences. One of the earliest writings on the Enneagram, as opined by Palmer and Wiltse is found in the book of Evagrius Ponticus in the 4th century. In his book, Ponticus gave eight personalities, which he called logismoi meaning "deadly thoughts" with the critical thought as "love of self." This was created because Ponticus thought that whatever one does as a judgment of another person's trait is influenced by the personality of that person.

In other words, people with the 'challenger' personality will mostly take 'enthusiasm' as a negative trait simply because they don't exhibit it. To bolster this, Ponticus further says that;

"The first thought of all is that love of self (Philautia); after this [come] the eight."

These identifications given by Ponticus caused a lot of commotion as people wondered how true it was to equate love to personalities. How could love originate without being altered too? In response to that, Ponticus gave the "remedies" to the eight thoughts. These solutions will be used to answer whatever questions that have to do with or would erupt on the ideas. With these remedies, many people saw the need to adopt the thoughts of Ponticus with all carefulness. Whether the resources given to the eight thoughts are still relevant in today's world is debatable.

The eight thoughts didn't, however, get enough publicity. But with the works of G.I. Gurdjieff, the Enneagram was known everywhere. This could have been the origin of what Enneagram is, alongside its study today. It is pertinent to note that Gurdjieff still retained the eight thoughts from Ponticus. As a matter of fact, they served as the guiding tenets of his work.

In modern day, Oscar Ichazo, a Bolivian, could be said to be Enneagram originator. The nine personality studies in this contemporary age are from his lectures, most importantly, those that focus on ego-fixations, virtues, passions, and holy ideas, delivered by Oscar in the 1950s. Another report claims that Oscar's well-detailed self-development and orientation were actually how he started the teaching that begot Enneagram. The lessons on 'Proto-analysis' uses the typical nine enneagram figures and ideas that are used today.

With the growth in awareness of Enneagram through Oscar's teaching, Africa institute based in Chile was established. However, it later moved to the United States of America when he relocated to South America. This is where the etymology of "Enneagram of Personality" can be traced to. Oscar later coined the term. As the enneagram personalities got enough establishments, Oscar needed to teach some of his students so that they would be able to take enneagram personalities around the globe and obviously to the next level.

In the 1970s, notable psychologists such as John Lilly and Claudio Naranjo went to Oscar to learn about the concept of Enneagram. Little wonder why these two were part of the earliest students of Oscar to understand Enneagram of personality. The Chilean and psychiatrist, Claudio Naranjo (from Arica in Chile) was in Africa Institute to take a course. Naranjo, having learned a great deal from Oscar, decided to start his teachings on Enneagram in the United States.

He took the teaching with a differing view from what his teacher, Oscar, taught him. He influenced some priest, the Jesuit, who adopted it to spiritual dealings. Enneagram took another approach against what Oscar wanted. His different approach, though friendly and straightforward, was perceived by Oscar as shrewd and misunderstanding. Because of this, Oscar disowned Naranjo and labeled his teachings as treacherous even though his lessons with other teachers spread like wildfire in the 1970s. Because Naranjo was teaching his understanding of Enneagram, his theory grew very fast and had students too.

As the saying goes, 'you shall reap what you sow,' Naranjo also witnessed the same thing he did to his teacher as his students also misconstrued and betrayed him in the end. Naranjo taught different things which were taken for spiritual dealings, and his students taught things that seemed to be more business inclined. Instead of preaching their teacher's teachings, they focus on a paradigm shift which saw them exploring the business side of Enneagram.

In the 1980s and 1990s, diverse authors such as Helen Palmer, Richard Rohr, Elizabeth Wagele and Don Richard Riso, started various publications on Enneagram. Meanwhile, the theories they taught and published are a mixture of how Enneagram erupted. In today's enneagram theories, attention to what the context of their application is, solely determined their usage and understanding. As part of the publishers, this book takes no particular view other than simplifying everything concerning Enneagram.

Maybe because enneagram founders understood and taught Enneagram at a different situation, many of Enneagram theories are basically on spirituality and business –as noted in the introduction. In fact, today, many authors would love to equate Enneagram to spirituality. This is very wrong, considering the history of the Enneagram. The account given here was confirmed from different authors and looking at it from different opinions. Enneagram is used in psychology and even neuroscience today. A lot of attention has been drawn to it because of how people have known about it lately.

Be that as it may, it is essential to know that the historical background of Enneagram follows an intricate pattern. From one scholar to another, from one philosopher to another, and from one teacher to another, the Enneagram concept had followed a fantastic design which had led to its rapid development over the past century. Additionally, the idea is still being transformed and developed with new ideas coming from young minds. Now, our next chapter will focus on where the concept of Enneagram was developed.

Chapter Three
Where Enneagram was developed

The exact nature of where Enneagram originated has been a mirage since its inception in the 4th century. As noted from the beginning of this book, contextual understanding of Enneagram has been developed through various conceptions and teachings from scholars with diverse ideas. Many people who published works to influence others on the nature of Enneagram never had the intention of the deduced meanings. Interestingly, one of the concepts of psychology that have suffered a lot of false conceptions is Enneagram.

Many people that start Enneagram do so with what could be considered diluted knowledge regarding where it was initially developed. Different conceptions of Enneagram have contributed immensely to what we know it as today. Here, the 'places' where Enneagram was developed are the most prominent ones throughout its history. They are where Enneagram can best be understood and found. They are the teachings of the notable more profound of the Enneagram personalities.

Since Enneagram has entertained different approaches and alarming concern from different professions –such as psychology, neurology, theology, and lots more –the need to understand where it was developed rose to some degree. It is pertinent to note that where Enneagram of personality developed from, as discussed here, is based on the diverse scholars of the Enneagram and not that there is a concrete building like a pyramid of Egypt or a monument center that begat it.

Additionally, Enneagrams development is based on the fact that there are different schools of thoughts with different terminologies. As well as approaches, conception, overlapping and merging, teachings, dealings, etc. The Enneagram we have today, though quite different from its original intention, is gotten from the places it evolved.

In past studies, psychologists have identified six basic 'places' where Enneagram originated. Keep in mind that this is different from the history of the Enneagram. The origins and places where it was developed to simplify the teachings of the developers. Below are the six 'places' where Enneagram was developed:

Don Richard Riso

Don Richard Riso is a neurotic approach to the study of the Enneagram. Its manner of dealing is to give a full description of the sequence in the nine personalities from the neurotic approach through to normal development and then to healthy emotion. The development of this kind of Enneagram was based on giving an analysis of how emotional health has evolved using the neurons in the body. Based on this approach and development, there have been many beliefs and teachings on this kind of Enneagram personality. It contributes to where the enneagram personality was developed.

Oscar Ichazo development of enneagram personalities

An approach that is based on Ichazo was developed in order to give the application of the nine personalities using varying schemata like ego and fixations in order to provide an analysis of self-development. Many books have used this approach where enneagram personalities had been developed both in the application and in actual teachings. The goal of the Enneagram in this approach is to provide the schema in self-development using the fixations theories.

Hameed A. Ali (A. S. Almaas) development of Enneagram personalities

Hameed A. Ali's development of Enneagram personalities is a psychological approach which evolved as another different kind of Enneagram. With this approach, Enneagram of personality is only a combination of studies from disciplines in the therapy of Gestalt through to that of Zen and the Reichian. It is purely psychological, thus studies the mind as well as how they affect human behavior. This particular type of Enneagram is probably the type that had received the most publications and teachings. This is likely due to the fact that it is one of the most fundamental things to humans –the mind. This has been considered as one of the comprehensive approaches to ascertain where the Enneagram of personalities has developed.

Claudio Naranjo development of enneagram personalities

Being a psychiatrist, Claudio proposed an approach that substitutes and replaces the usage of neurotic terms and strategies with psychiatric jargons and dealings. The total reliance on neurotic usage of transactions as a determinant of Enneagram personality was denounced and changed. Essentially, everything boiled down to the psychiatric approach. Well, because this approach is more or less synonymous to the disorder of human, and this is why many people reject it for a better approach – meanwhile only those within the field love to use it. Whenever you read a book relating to Enneagram that utilizes this kind of personality developed, adjust your attention to their terminologies only.

Helen Palmer

Helen Palmer is the sort of Enneagram that focuses on the overall narrative of prevalent teachings. Just like this book, this development is in learning the general idea as there is no particular niche given. On a closing note, this Enneagram developed here is based on the teachings and approaches it had from its inception. It is not to nullify that Enneagram is based on the nine human personalities in their social relations and reactions to things and people. Based on this general background, it is believed that the development of Enneagram is from the first developer.

Oscar Ichazo development of Enneagram personalities

The Oscar Ichazo development is an approach that was developed as a way to give the application of the nine personalities, through the use of varying schemata,ego, for example. Psychologists and other great developers of Enneagram have agreed, at least to some extent, that those enneagram personalities had been in man since childbirth. Noting that there were not many new insights found when they traced the origin of the Enneagram to inhuman sources. In fact, the only thing that was discovered was the naming, description, and teachings of the nine Enneagram personalities which have been believed to be an influence of different developers explained at the beginning of this chapter. The line of enneagram development is evolving, and the probability of having much more approaches in the future is very high.

Lastly, note that the development of Enneagram has followed several approaches; however, none has ruled out the context of birth in the perception of the concept by the developer. This is one of the reasons enneagram personalities have many misconceptions even from the onset. The approach given here is the underlying factor which proves that Enneagram is a model and also a system of nine human personalities, using the names mostly adopted and not the popularly known misconception because this book will give you a complete introduction to the Enneagram personalities.

This chapter should familiarize you with the knowledge of the different school of thoughts in regards to the Enneagram. Having a deep understanding of where the concept originated from would also go a long way in putting you through a straight path concerning this journey. This chapter will help broaden your horizon as regards this concept. Now, which Enneagram school do you fancy? Which do you find appealing? Once you lay this foundation, the rest will fall into place.

Chapter Four
Why choose Enneagram and what are the benefits you can get from it?

Either consciously or unconsciously, we must have shown or exuded a particular character that must have put us within a circle of those nine personalities. These nine personalities help us shape our lives for the better, as they allow us to alter and improve our interactions with the world. The knowledge we acquire through Enneagram helps us to understand with more experience about what the world is all about. Additionally, it helps us understand our emotional reactions and how to defend our behavior, the behavior of others, our highest qualities, and our purpose in life.

The new world order focuses on the interaction between us. Thanks to globalization, we can no longer stay in a state of autarky even if we really want to. Enneagram allows us to focus our energy into making sure these interactions between ourselves are fostered and improved in every way. Instead of being dependent on our emotions and following the dictates of these many emotions that we tend to feel in regard to our relationships with others. Enneagram would give us the power to stay aware and in control of these emotions and in turn, understand the personality of any individuals we are interacting with. That way, we would achieve success, motivation, and attention in the long run.

Ask yourself, are you finding it extremely difficult to have a long-term relationship? Are your connections with your friends and families strained as a result of misconception or an emotional breakdown? Are you finding it difficult to understand and relate with the people around you, either at home or your workplace? If so, then this chapter is for you. Immerse yourself in it and make sure you digest every word to the best of your abilities.

There are different benefits to Enneagram, but here we will only focus on some of the more prominent ones. The Enneagram or the study of personality can help you on a personal level and in your relationships too. It can also help people in their professions and businesses.

Also, the Enneagram equips us with the appropriate tools to bring about profound change within ourselves so that we can bring a balance to our lives. It helps us keep clear thoughts and straight heads so that we can conquer the problems of our lives instead of being consumed by them. The benefits stated here are based on the general usage and understanding of Enneagram. They include:

- Adequate awareness of people's personalities in the world no matter how unconventional:

Beyond your experience in life, Enneagram makes you aware of how people could behave. For example, in an unfamiliar community, the knowledge of enneagram personalities help to create an awareness of the possible behavior patterns you may encounter. That way, you will be able to see beyond our your own limited experiences and perceptions. In other words, knowing other people's personality as well as yours makes relating to people more comfortable. With this awareness, it is easier to live our lives fully and also maintain a healthier relationship.

- Successful relationships in all ramifications:

Using Enneagram would undoubtedly make sure that the relationships that you keep both at work and at home are a success. This is true because by understanding our own unconscious reactions to situations, we can be more understanding and flexible when dealing with other people's responses to similar situations. Thus, allowing us to see it as normal for people to react to actions. We would equally develop a well-prepared mind and compassion to whatever their behavior turns out to be.

- Enhancing tolerance

With the knowledge of Enneagram, you are able to be aware of what people will likely say. Thus you take things less personally. When you know your personality type, it is easier to relate, and when there is a problem, you will be able to handle it with caution knowing full well that you could have handled it the same way or worse. The negative feeling you get when people treat you negatively would have less of an impact on you and become less painful to you. This is because you are now aware of their personalities. Your tolerance is heightened because you understand the decision-making processes of various kinds of personalities.

- <u>Rapid personal growth:</u>

Being able to identify the different types of personalities through Enneagram involves taking an in-depth look at the emotion, and the psychology of them, as well as how they allow us to grow beyond measures. After all, self-awareness leads to personal development and empathy in the judgment of others. When you possess the ability to develop your mental and emotional strength because you have a complete understanding of your personality and development, you are able to handle the challenges that come from dealing with people a lot better. Many positive changes can be expected as the ability to harness your personality traits develops and grows. In general, intellectual development is achieved during the process of coming to terms with one's personality and managing its accompanying challenges.

- <u>Improvement of positive thinking</u>

It doesn't matter who you are, once you understand the Enneagram personalities and their traits your mindset will change. You will experience a change in how negative reactions that you encounter impact your relationships because you're already aware of and familiar with their personality. You will live with less doubt and skepticism because you are more informed about actions and reactions. And, you will be at peace with everyone around because they are more comfortable with you based on the fact that you understand them.

- <u>Adequate management of challenging relationships:</u>

There are always situations where people of different minds come together to share ideas. With an understanding of Enneagram, you will be able to manage anyone's feelings about any situation that arises. Once you identify your personality type, and you know the strengths and weaknesses you possess, you will be able to interact with people of different personality types more effectively and healthily. The way they view things might be different from yours but with correct handling and management, opposing and challenging people of varying personality types can be successfully managed. You will build an immune system that helps you manage opposing behaviors from your colleagues at work because of the understanding of Enneagram personalities.

- <u>Helps with parenting</u>

While parenting can be an incredibly difficult task, with the knowledge of Enneagram, parents are able to demystify children's personalities and improve understanding. The way in which children change as they grow and develop can be better understood, allowing the parent/child relationship to strengthen when it often becomes more challenging. This is because children have the ability to exhibit multiple personality types within the same year. Not only that, but parent's personalities can differ from their children's greatly. However, understanding the Enneagram makes it easier for parents to know how to relate with them. This is why parents have found Enneagram very interesting –much of what it is about will be discussed later in this book.

- <u>Enhancing recognition of both emotional and physical needs</u>

Through the study of the Enneagram, everyone is aware of the need to maintain healthy, physical, and emotional needs plus care. People will take more care not to be a source of emotional unbalance. With the understanding of who you are and your flaws, you will be able to understand what you need at any given time. People of shy personalities or the personality type of Investigators -who love confinement-, will know how to manage their behaviors. They will know when to be confined and when to mix and relate with others. Enneagram personalities would keep affected and educated people abreast with the fact that emotions are one of the primary things that make up a person.

- Ability to avoid dispute

With the help of mutual understanding of enneagram personalities, conflict rates are reduced significantly among people. This is not because these series of misunderstandings won't occur. As a matter of fact, they will definitely come through no matter how little some of them are. However, the fact that there is background knowledge of what the personalities involved are would undoubtedly make these misunderstandings easier to manage and deal with.

The understanding of Enneagram could be more beneficial to people within the same business patterns. More so, gatherings, where opinions are solicited, would find Enneagram very relevant and helpful. The nature of the conflict is a bridge in normalcy and abnormality of things. Thus, solving and finding common ground as regards this conflict would see to the success and development of a relationship. That said, if people can have the same perception of things, there is a great tendency, they react in the same way.

Well there you have it, a few of the outstanding benefits you stand to gain from the Enneagram. Believe it or not, your life would be far better with Enneagram in it. When you practice this particular concept in your life, you are bound to enjoy blissfulness and blessedness. So what are you waiting for?

In conclusion, the reasons and benefits of Enneagram are felt most when you understand the context of its usage. Enneagram understanding creates a wide range of peace and harmonious co-existence in all ramifications, especially in the life of those working side-by-side with one another. Take advantage of the knowledge of Enneagram, and improve your life!

Chapter Five
The first personality

In the scale of the nine personalities, the first one has different names such as the idealist, the reformer, the perfectionist, the purpose-driven, the principled, and the self-controlled. This might be because of the context of usage. The critical thing to remember is that they all mean the same thing. The term to be used in this chapter is that of the reformer. They are given these names because of their love of making anything they are involved in better. They are perfectionists who strive to make order out of everything regardless of how chaotic. They strive to be perfect, and when unable to be that, they do their best to try and strike a balance. This is because they love being remembered for good deeds.

The Description of the Reformer

The reformer loves to be viewed as without faults and is very good at keeping their morals in check. The bearer of this personality has good ethics. As well as a high priority of doing the right things and differentiating the wrong. They always try with utmost carefulness to avoid mistakes in order for people not to scold them or be disappointed. People with this personality are very noble, wise, and realistic in every situation.

They could be regarded as people-pleasers –always wanting to be right in the sight of others. Though they have the problem of inadequate patience while doing things, their comportment and maintenance of excellence, high standards and orderliness are part of what makes them unique. People who fall into this category are always orderly and organized, and dislike anyone that is less organized and thus are tagged perfectionists. In short, everything must be perfect for them no matter the situation.

Reformers put in a lot time correcting people which in turn, is why they detest being corrected themselves. The majority of the time, they avoid and complain about people that lag in their responsibilities, often they will be the ones to actually take note of this the fastest. Because they always love to shape the world around them to suit their needs and desires, they are often seen as social reformers. Reformers also tend to have a keen eye for detail and can notice when things are wrong, out of place, or not in a situation of perfection.

A fascinating fact about this personality type, perhaps true of others too, is that they have what drives them to behave and react this way –having a fear of being remembered for wrong deeds. They are always scared of doing wrong because they have infallible trust and integrity, appear to be accurate in all things, and so on. Everything and anything can motivate them. They are pushed by their desire to be the best among people, have a feeling of no guilt, improve in everything they do, and avoiding correction from people.

They're teachers at every point. Their ideals push them around with sincerity and strength. Funny enough, no matter how they grow, they love to accommodate people's view about things and admittance of the imperfectness in them. The motto of a reformer is "change what can be changed, about those that can't be changed, develop wisdom and tricks to know the difference between these things." They can be very resentful, however, whenever they get angry. They always know that "I am a responsible and objective person" –they barely deviate from this.

There are some things that reformers are used to, as well as a number of things that they can often be found doing. Below are some of the things they are well known for:

- Cleanliness and order

Their surroundings have to be spotless and well arranged. When they are not reformers are generally uncomfortable and uneasy. Most of the time, when things are not done in accordance with how they would prefer, those who fall into this personality group start to criticize. In order to affirm the existence of Enneagram, many scholars have given examples of each personality. Notable examples of reformers are Noam Chomsky, Confucius, Osama bin Laden, Celine Dion, Hillary Clinton, Plato George F. Will, Justice Sandra

Day O'Connor, Nelson Mandela, etc. Some, although uncommon, have a mixture of reformer personality –it might not be the full one.

- They hate lies and dishonesty

If there is one thing that reformers truly detest it is liars and dishonest people. As much as a reformer tends to behave as a perfectionist in all things, they still won't stoop low to indulge themselves in dishonest dealings. This might even make a reformer break total ties with you completely.

- They always want to do things their own way

This is one of the attributes that makes them a perfectionist. A perfectionist will never bend nor will they sway from their beliefs, opinion, and ideas no matter how wrong they might turn out to be. They simply want things to be done in their own way. All perfectionists want to be head of a campaign or crusade no matter how shrewd it may seem. They just want to take the lead in anything they do. And no matter how wrong they might seem, other people's opinion doesn't really matter to them so long they end up achieving their own objective.

How to improve as a reformer

- Be patient

It is not uncommon for reformers who feel that they have done their best to better the people around them to realize that those people remain unmoved or unchanged. Often leaving the reformers to feel discouraged. When this happens, the best thing you can do is to exercise some patience. That you have done your very best, but ultimately cannot control another person's actions. It is more relieving and better not to be perfect at everything as there is always going to be a way around things.

Give them time to acculturate those things you want them to do – time heals all things. Your good deed will surely pay off in the lives of others. You're always a teacher; expecting behavioral changes in your 'students' will be an utmost concern to you, but in the end, always be patient.

- Reduce your harshness

Because you don't want people to see your faults, you get harder on yourself. Sometimes, you find yourself worrying over little things, especially after you've done something wrong and harmful to others around you. Don't punish yourself too much; you are human, after all. The way you'd do to others you see in the 'wrong' acts is what you do on yourself. The self-irritations you develop can barely solve the problem, and being friendly with people makes things easier. Understand yourself by considering those things that irritate you and device a better approach to dealing with them, so they do not get to you as much.

- Make sure you have enough time to relax

As much as reformers tend to always be on the go, it is crucial to know that the body needs rest too. Sometimes, reformers tend to go overboard in satisfying the need of everyone around them no matter the consequences. Additionally, they also put in more effort into making sure things go in order even if it means over stressing the body to achieve it. We should know that our body needs to rest in order to function well. Thus, keep your body fresh and healthy at all times. That is the only way you can achieve everything that you have planned.

- Know you are human too

Even if you fall into the reformer category - you are not a robot. It would do you a lot of good if you can keep this in mind at all times. No matter how hard you try to control your emotions, you would still come to terms with the fact that we cannot control our feelings. If at all, we can manage it, then it is only the outcome of our emotions that we can take control of. Additionally, we should also have it at the back of our mind that no matter how hard we try to be perfect, there are still going to be traces of imperfection around us. Don't feel bad when this happens. Don't get down on yourself when you start experiencing these kind of errors in your perfect life. Don't let it weigh you down.

In conclusion, reformers strive to do the right things. It is a compulsion they feel from the core of their being. They love everybody to have a high opinion of themselves, even though this is impossible. The reformers are perfectionists, and as such, they always want to be perfect in everything they do. This is the life of a reformer explained.

Now ask yourself if this is where you belong. Ask yourself if this particular personality fits your description. And if it does, then you should follow the various ways we listed above, on improving yourself. That is the only way you will be able to adjust with other personality types. But if you don't quite fit this personality type, don't worry. There are still eight more personality types, as you will see you in the next chapter.

Chapter Six
The second personality

In this chapter, we are going to focus on the second of the nine personality types - the helpers. This personality is also commonly referred to as the lover personality.

People with this personality are typically caring and generous and gain a strong sense of worth when they offer aid or assistance to people in any way. In some ways, it is as though they exist to assist and derive pride from helping. In some ways, it is as though they feel a sense of responsibility any time they are around others. That way, they would be given the overall praises in the end.

The description of the Helpers

Helpers are easy to befriend because they are kind-hearted, opened, sincere, and loving. They can sacrifice anything for anyone, regardless of the circumstances. And are commonly considered to be people-pleasers who can be sentimental in the judgment of people around them. Their love for people is unquantifiable; they love to the extreme.

This personality is referred to as the helper because they will often go out of their way to help to the point that it is at their detriment. Their concern for people makes them experience life in its entirety. One of the primary problems that helpers face is that they often fail to admit their own needs because of others. People with this personality are incredibly emotional and quickly feel empathy, which makes them more prone to understanding others and knowing what to do to help.

In short, they live a sort of sacrificial life, to the point that often people wonder why and how they do some things for others without being compensated. This could be because they don't want to be found unworthy of love and of being loved and simply have a need to be loved by everyone. They wish to show how they feel towards everyone around them.

Essentially, when the helpers help, they want people's response of appreciation –this is one of their primary driving forces. They care about people and wish to establish this truth about themselves. Amazingly, the helpers consider their ability to forgo their own way of doing things in order to satisfy people as the noblest life of a person; thus, they invest much of their time in doing so.

Have you ever noticed how some people have natural parental-like characteristics? They want to know how you've been faring, to recognize and appreciate you. They help you not only see but encourage you to embrace those qualities and attributes hidden in you so that you can learn and grow. Often people with these characteristics are able to let go of grudges, regardless of how bad the situation or experience might have been; instead, they love to help people see how to improve. When you observe these people, their lives are consecrated to showing people love. They do everything for love, and that is what makes them lovers.

There are many people known for this personality, but notable among them are Dolly Parton, Nancy Reagan, Paramahansa Yogananda, Paula Abdul, Barry Manilow, Mary Kay Ash, Kenny G., Jennifer Tilly, Stevie Wonder, Elizabeth Taylor, Danny Thomas, and Bishop Desmond Tutu, etc.

Reasons Helpers are always willing to offer their services

- Empathy and emotion

The ease with which they feel other people's feelings and needs enable them to understand when and why people need their help. People with this personality also pity people easily and are always ready and willing to assist when needed. Empathy is the watchword of every lover out there because that is the only pathway they know in connecting with the people around them. Additionally, people who fall into this personality are emotional beings. At the slightest thing, they would feel a surge of emotions towards anyone that needs their help, and the empathy in them would further push them towards lending a helping hand. More like empathy and feelings are what drive them.

- Pride

People of this second personality derive a sense of pride when they are successful in helping people in any way. Although they pity people and are always willing, they feel proud when they eventually give help. When they help people, they expect gratitude for the extent to which they went to offer assistance. The feeling that comes after lending a helping hand to others can sometimes overwhelm the lovers. At a particular time, they would want to feel this way all over again, thereby making them extend their helping hand anytime and any day.

- Love Expectations

On the dark side of people with the second personality, is that they fear that no matter how much they give, they will never receive the love they deserve in return. This often leads them to have low self-esteem. It propels them to do more, regardless of what that entails. They love it when people hail them for doing things and always look forward to an acknowledgment when they do good things. Nothing beats the feeling of being loved by as many people as possible. This is one of the primary reasons why lovers don't mind inconveniencing themselves for others. Getting an appraisal and heap of love from the people around them is enough to make them feel special even while hurting.

<u>Challenges facing helpers include:</u>

- Pride:

This pride is associated with self-worth, which is solely derived from having people always seeking opinions and also consulting them on life's challenges. They think the ability to attend to every persons situation makes them the best. Though this could be based on love at the onset, it may develop into pride later while attending to people. It should be noted that they love being praised.

- Over-involvement in life:

Because helpers are seen as being good friends, many of them are faced with the challenge of involving themselves in the lives of people too much. They believe that helping people and getting involved in people's lives is a way of maintaining their self-worth.

- Using manipulative methods:

Helpers always want to know people's feeling about specific issues. So, whenever they are with someone, they keep their emotions to themselves. Helpers will use manipulative methods to get through and satisfy their needs. Most of them even forget that the lives of people do not revolve around them, and they barely understand that how people end up living their lives is outside their control. They manipulate the thoughts of people and infuse theirs in order to satisfy their emotional needs –helping people.

After all their challenges, helpers love to binge on carbohydrate food and sweet things like sugar a lot. They often abuse food no matter how little the availability. They do counter medications too. As if those aren't enough, helpers, because of having the feeling of love deprivation, overeat to ease themselves. Helpers also have the ability to fake emotions in order to look for sympathy at all cost.

Developers of the Enneagram have developed the development of the helper personality. The remedies are what helpers can do or avoid in order to improve. If you've identified yourself with the descriptions given above, do the following:

Attending to yourself first

The truth is that without a thorough understanding of you first, attending to people with the same problem will be very difficult –the best teacher is an experience. If this sounds like you, then the first thing to do in order to improve is to get to know yourself properly. This isn't because of selfishness; it is just carefulness and common sense. You don't want to talk about things that you have less experience or knowledge about. Try everything in your power to attend to your own issues and needs first before others'. In a bid to attend to people, you must learn to take enough rest and care of yourself adequately. With this, healthy growth is bound to happen.

Knowing the needs of targeted people

Based on the fact that you'll be helping people, understanding and identifying their needs should be your utmost priority. When you know their needs, attending to them adequately, timely and satisfactorily is easier and more effective. You can't assume that your needs are the same as other people's. Try to know what their needs are to be more relevant to them. Ask them what they need and how they'd like them to be fulfilled. Tell them that you want to help and be prepared for people to turn you down. That people tell you they don't need your help at a particular time doesn't mean they wouldn't need you later. Don't feel rejected or dejected; there will always be some other people will need your help.

Be a good receiver of love

In order to improve your dealings with others, you have to be more receptive to kind wishes and love from people too. You don't have to know the gesture, but it is vital that you try to recognize when people are showing love to you and appreciate it more. Being a good receiver of love promotes the way you show love to people because you understand what it means to be loved. Bear in mind that love is always available at every point; the only thing that determines how we feel it is our reaction to it.

Establish your motives

Many people could even feel insecure while you're trying to help them. The best thing to do is to make your motives known to the person. Remember that you are helping people and as such, you would love to receive some compensation. If you start with your established and well-known goals, the person will appreciate you even more. Don't do random help; know what is applicable in different situations you come across.

Avoid eye-service

As long as it is good to know people for their excellent work, avoid proclamation of your good deeds by yourself. Don't call people's attention to what you've done to get more appreciation for the job done. When you help people, whether the person recognizes you or not should not bother you. The danger of calling people's attention is that they'll be uncomfortable –this is normal to everyone and everywhere –because they feel you're intimidating them. This kind of behavior will not make you grow, nor will it promote your relationship with the people around you. This could affect you to the extent of seeing even your good deeds as a way to put you in the spotlight.

Additionally, being a person with this personality is a wonderful personality to hold. This only shows you have a kind and selfless heart. However, you should be more concerned about yourself first before any other person. The reason why I'm stressing this point is not to push you away from your inner self. Our inner self has the ability to recognize our true self. With that said, when pride starts setting in when you start doing things selfishly, and when you begin showing eye service to get the love of others, going back to your inner self is paramount and inevitable. That is the only way you can actually regain touch with your real lover's personality.

In conclusion, the helpers are loving and fun. Many people cherish and wish to have this personality as it is one of the ways to live a healthy life. The helpers are like the messiah of many people because they always love to watch people become the best version of themselves. If you have these descriptions, consider everything and stop acting like a greenhorn. Make life better for you by understanding who you are on a deep level –don't be a shadow of yourself. The helpers are some of the best people. The next chapter would delve into the third personality; why don't you turn the page over?

Chapter Seven
The Third Personality

As a beginner in the world of Enneagram, these different and diverse personalities might sound a bit strange to you. If this is the case, there is no need to panic. It is completely normal. I was once in your shoes, years ago, when I was first getting started. But as I learned more and began to identify the various personality traits that I possess, it all began to fall into place.

So, you don't identify with either the reformer or lover personalities? Perhaps you are more of an Achiever. Now, I know, you are probably asking who these Achievers are? This is the third personality trait we will look at. Other names given to them are; result-oriented, success-driven, pragmatic, and adaptable. They are given these names because of their need for success in various endeavors. Whatever field they find themselves in, they strive for success in order to build their level of self-worth.

The description of the Achievers

People with this kind of personality are typically described as charming, energetic, attractive, and elegant. In whatever they do, their competence drives them to excellence. Where many people would usually be nonchalant about development and class, achievers are always conscious of it. They are incredibly diplomatic and tactical in their approach to things because their concern is to achieve success all the time.

In the mind of an achiever, failure is essentially the worst thing on earth, which is precisely why they would use all their power to hit every challenge to achieve the desired results; success. Things that could draw achievers back while aiming at a particular challenge are their concerning thoughts on how people will perceive them and the kind of image that they might portray. Because of their drive to succeed, people with these traits, have an incredibly competitive mind, and those who can work all the time are their greatest threat.

In fact, they would, by all means, avoid them because they feel that they create a kind of stress for them. In some ways, achievers dealing with competition is equivalent to them beating the shadows of themselves. Achievers are also a source of good inspiration to the people around them.

They are scared of being irrelevant and worthless. They also try to be the best at doing a particular thing; they always want to retain that position no matter the circumstances. They will go to any length in order to achieve their success. All that they want is to be valuable and worthy of everything in their name. They avoid any kind of venture that is likely to fail because this would hurt them very badly.

It isn't as though they wouldn't attempt a new venture, but whatever they decide to try has to be something they are sure to succeed at. People with this personality trait are professionals at everything they do. Achievers always want to be confirmed as the best especially if people doubt how excellent they could they could be a something. They often stand out from the crowd with great distinction. Most importantly, achievers want attention.

They work best when receiving praise as opposed to condemnation. Admiration is part of what drives achievers in whatever they do – people must admire excellence. Funny enough, achievers don't just work for people, they want to impress them. No matter how trivial that thing is, achievers are always out to impress others, especially those in a supervisory role. When they do not get recognition, they can be dejected for days. The majority of people who fall into this personality type will not feel like working anymore and want to resign. This is their weakness; rejection from people.

The name given to this category is premised on the fact that these people can aim at anything in life and achieve success. Because of their achievements, many people look up to them as models of the human race. This is actually their aim too. They are aware of the contribution of humans to the world, so they do everything to develop themselves and also to motivate people around them.

Achievers are always selected as representatives of people wherever they find themselves. Many people take it as goodwill to use achievers as the representatives because of excellence, motivation, and achievements. Some of them have been leading their class from childhood. They wouldn't force it; it is what people want. Achievers are always the standout and leader of the group.

The achievers are regarded as the most loved among other types of the Enneagram personalities. They are the role models for a lot of people of their own enneagram personality and the other eight as well. They are living legends because of their records which have to fend them the social value they desire. They spend most of their time doing what they can do best. With this development, many are given adequate inspiration to build themselves, as their mentors are doing so too.

There is this special thing about the achievers: attaining success based on what their communities call it. In one place, being successful could be tied to having material things such as cars, houses, etc. In another place, it could be the ability to birth great and feasible ideas. Whatever the prerequisites, achievers will always get their desire, success. They still want to leave a legacy of success behind them; this is part of their drive.

Even when achievers are young, they love to focus on those impossible things they met as history in order to beat it and lead among their families. No matter the price of being the best and of excellence, the achievers are ready to pay it. They can't just be anybody without a name. Most of them are reckoned within their communities, nations, states, and countries. When their names are mentioned, they save lives and properties. Achievers will surely buy affluence for their families, both nuclear and extended. They are the heroes of our time, and most times, their achievement records are unbeatable. This is their goal.

Achievers do not aim for success for any reason other than their fear of been forgotten after their death. They put everything together to be remembered forever in their residence. There is no special dividend expected from the people achievers are helping; they just want them to proclaim their names around the world. People must speak of their achievements and prowess through the ages.

A lot of people with the "achiever" personality trait, are quite addicted to some things because of their success orientation and drive. They can starve themselves when on the mission of achievement. They hardly take time to rest, and they work till their body is completely exhausted. Some of them get addicted to drugs such as cocaine, to stimulate themselves. Whatever the addiction, they barely see it as bad once they attain the fame they want.

There are great people known for this kind personality. They might not have been, entirely, bearing this personality but have a touch of it. Some of them are Bill Clinton, Justin Bieber, Courtney Cox, Michael Jordan, Augustus Caesar, Werner Erhard, Paul McCartney, Whitney Houston, Reese Witherspoon, Richard Gere, Dick Clark, Chef Daniel Boulud, Tony Robbins, Ken Watanabe, etc.

There is nothing without its disadvantages; the same applies to the achiever personality. They face a few challenges given below:

The tendency to lose themselves

Achievers desire to be the best in spite of all odds. With this desire, they tend to lose their authentic self because they leave out very little time to take care of themselves. They are subject to the deception of fame and achievement. Usually, because achievers tend to chase glory from their childhood, they lose themselves even before they know themselves. This is so sad, but it's the truth.

Lack of feeling

Achievers are purely active people; they barely have time for feelings. It is as bad as not paying attention to whatever is happening around them. They don't have or hardly feel people's emotions. It is as if their feelings have separated from them. When things happen to them, they appear to be numbed and barely take it the way other people do. So far, their achievements are attained; whatever negative feelings were induced scarcely concerns them.

Lack of focus

Many achievers don't really know what they want. All they do is to satisfy the desires of others. Their numbed attitudes towards feelings could be because they believe that since they would enjoy the gain, they should endure the pain too. Achievers don't have a great focus; they only want achievements and records. Their aim for fame blinds their eyes.

Having stated the possible challenges of achievers, it is necessary to give some ways to overcome these challenges. Achievers could develop and grow in the following few ways:

Create and accept your own needs and feeling

To grow as an achiever, you have to learn how to succumb to your feelings. Whenever you're exhausted, be truthful to yourself; take enough time to rest. The achievements that you're always running after are not equivalent to your life. People wouldn't love you less simply because you took some time off. Avoid faking your feelings. You are human, and it is normal to get tired.

Learn how to give yourself time

This isn't saying that you should neglect your goals and sleep all day; it merely means that you need to take time to regain strength and not exhaust yourself. You would be surprised what a thirty-minute nap would do for you. You should also practice taking things slow and taking time to think things through. Take enough rest and achieve your dreams; nobody is in competition with you; after all, they can't understand your own approach.

Resist doing the acceptable

Achievers always want to do things that are acceptable to others at their own detriment. It is about time you resisted the feeling to please people and focus on your needs. This is critical to living a happy life. Sometimes, it is fine not to do things that will satisfy people. As long as it doesn't hurt anyone adversely, do things you want to do because you want to do them.

Strengthen your relationships

If you must exhaust yourself in order to meet your goals, try to take out time to discuss and strengthen your relations with the people in your life. You can't always tell everyone you're busy all the time. Your family and friends should get some of your time too. You will do this consciously by giving yourself the time to work and also devote time to your friends and family. Remember that both your death and life are affected by them. Give them your life before they have to accept your death.

Work on your own goals

Usually, the achiever's fame comes from helping others with their plans. The truth is that when you work on your personal goals, you have more chances of earning better achievements. By doing so, you will achieve not only fame but also happiness that comes from the fulfillment of your goals. A real legacy is achieved when your life's work was for you and not someone else. This is what could be referred to as an achievement.

In conclusion, achievers are one of the best of the enneagram personalities and ironically, suffer more than the others as well. They're true heroes. Nevertheless, there is always time for everything. Time to be everyone's hero and also time to watch out for yourself. What is the gain of an achiever if he or she saves the day and ends up losing his or herself? Thus, as an achiever, you need to be steadfast, you need to be cautious, and you need to be thoughtful too. That is the only way you can achieve real success in the world. The next chapter promises to be much more captivating and intriguing. Stay with us as we unravel the next personality trait – the Individualist.

Chapter Eight
The Fourth personality

It is essential to know that among the nine Enneagram personalities, the fourth is primarily known as the individualist. Like every other type whose numerous names may have developed because of the subject matter (Enneagram), the individualists are also sometimes known as being the dramatic, the sensitive, and the outspoken. People of this personality type see themselves as different from others. They view this difference as something that ought to be embraced and are proud of it. However, at the same time - they loathe it.

The description of Individualists

Many people perceive individualists as insignificant because a lot of the time, their identity is not really known by anyone. People who fall into this category are reserved and barely talk among people as they prefer to keep their thoughts and opinions to themselves. One thing about these people is that they are always aware of themselves, no matter what situations they might find themselves in. Individualists are very sensitive to things and are able to note negative behaviors in people quickly.

Honesty is vital to the individualist. They are also prone to be quite moody. People with this personality trait enjoy solitude and derive pleasure from keeping to themselves. The individualists could be in a place for a long time, and people will barely notice them. They love to withdraw themselves from people because of their feeling of the defect. Sometimes, an individualist might develop negative feelings about people or situations, and this causes them to withdraw and choose to be on their own. They are very creative in whatever job or work they are given.

One of the most significant issues with the individualists is that they tend to pity themselves and are melancholic. Their primary goal is to be significant, but they end up without the significance they seek.

They want to give their own opinions at all times. Individualists are very happy when they see the beauty in things and are devoted to emotional dealings; they abstain from anything that will break them. It is said that they are very sensitive. However, their emotions are hard to decipher. As much as they desire being understood, people barely ever truly understand them.

Individualists are also usually quite quick to admit that their personality is different from others. Where most people enjoy being social individualists, they actually revel in solitude and love to be alone. Besides this, they always think that they have unique qualities and talents and can be one of the best if given a chance. They believe that being unfortunate is the worst thing in life. People who fall into this category love to focus on their strengths, and barely care about what people think about them.

One fantastic thing about this trait is that it happens to be a personality with the best appraisal of themselves. They will give an analysis of what they can and can't do without withholding any truth. They live in their own facts no matter what their judgment is. They'll show the world that dark side of them with the aim of knowing those that are for or against them. Mercifully, the individualists' complete understanding of their true self makes it easy for them to empathize with other personality types, thereby having the ability to live peacefully with them.

Individualists are also often on the lookout for whatever they see in themselves in others. They also tend to worry about both significant and minor details. Whenever doubt creeps into their mind it can often result in some of them feeling they aren't good enough at anything.

Though individualists appear less social, they really want to be with people and socialize. They are believed, by enneagram scholars, to be the most romantic of all nine personalities. They want people to come close in order to discover and appreciate their personality. Many people will refer to them as hypocrites because, in many ways, people within this group are the opposite of who they want to be. For example, an individualist may desire to be the best drummer. They may even have some talent for drumming, but the lack of diligence at rehearsals will ensure they never reach that goal. They prefer to live in a fantasy. When people notice this ability in them, they're always ashamed of themselves even though they will do little or nothing about it. Because of this, individualist will try their utmost to invent who they aren't. Though unsatisfied, individualists will always want to test whether they could be another person.

The issue is that they let their fluctuating feelings control them and their actions. They always portray a shadow of who they actually are. Because of this, they nurse low self-esteem. They have one significant challenge: they can barely let go of their past. Coupled with low self-esteem, they allow bad experiences in the past or present to affect their judgment and dealings with people. The worst is seen when the experiences are terrible.

There are different things that individualists tend to do often because of their nature. Individualists do these things and are addicted to them. Some of those things include constant depression, where they often binge on sweet things alongside food. They are extremist at socializing and have a bad habit of taking things to the max, for example, taking too much Tobacco when they are emotionally down or alcohol to brighten their mood.

There are different things individualists can do to develop themselves. They could do the following to improve on themselves:

- <u>Less attention to feelings</u>

Within the description, it is evident that emotions are what inspire you to do whatever you do. Many times things look good, but upon recalling negative thoughts, you're down again. This needs to stop. Develop a kind of immunity against it by knowing and accepting that these feelings get to you. Work on them if you can change them, otherwise, let things go. Using your emotions to judge what you do will mar everything. Desist from it.

- Don't use imaginative thoughts

Many times, you've thought about and judged everything even before they happened. It is as if you're expecting things to work out negatively, as they seem to do generally. Things aren't always the way you see them. You may need to fix your mindset. Thinking about things before they happen is alright, but do not expect them always to turn out bad. That is only the past affecting the present.

- Stay away from the 'right mood' hypothesis

There are many times, as an individualist, your actions are needed, but you put them off until the right mood comes. This will affect your reaction to things, there is a right time to do things, and it is not necessarily when you feel like it. To act at a different time may be equivalent to putting in the effort where it is no longer needed. Do what needs to be done when it needs to be done.

- Self-discipline

Building good self-discipline is vital as an individualist. This means that all those harmful addictions will need to be kept under control as they are the significant contributors to the negative feelings you get at every point. Think of a way to go around things rather than trying to play 'safe' by doing bad things to ease you off things. This is affecting your coexistence with other people. With self-discipline, you are ready for improvement. Note that this wouldn't come once; discipline is inculcated with time.

- Build enough self-esteem

It should come as no surprise that as humans, we work best when we feel confident and have good self-esteem. Regardless of who you are low self-esteem gets the mind weary and incapable, negatively impacting your ability to perform at your optimal level. In order to develop, you must learn to step your esteem up. Building good esteem is just doing things that suit you without worrying about what others are thinking or will feel about them. By doing this, you will experience growth in your self-esteem.

This will also help you realize that people are also not as bad as you have commonly painted them to be. If there is one thing individualists are good at, it is being loyal. An individualist would stay with you through thick or thin as they mostly cherish their friendships. Now, doesn't that sound better than being friends with someone who leaves when life inevitably gets tough?

The next chapter will focus on the fifth personality. If you haven't seen yourself in any of the personalities that we've already looked at, this upcoming personality might just be for you.

Chapter Nine
The Fifth Personality

The fifth personality of the Enneagram is the investigator. Just as the name depicts, investigators are primarily people who find themselves wanting to get to the root of every matter no matter how irrelevant it may seem. They are pushed with a particular drive to know things first hand. Other names, such as innovative thinkers have been given to them. The investigator personality is given its name because more than any other character, they want to find out why things are the way they are.

The description of the fifth personality

People who fall into this personality category truly value knowledge. They pursue expertise in viewing the world objectively and enjoy in-depth studies of how things work. Investigators are motivated to spend a lot of time learning about objective studies and analytical thinking in order to make well-informed decisions and conclusions. They tend to challenge the opinion of others and find out facts about a topic.

Investigators are typically described as eccentric in the observation and research of things. Although not everyone in this category is drawn to academic brilliance, they also have a tendency to be slightly weird and irregular in their thinking. However, whichever field they choose they tend to become experts and excel at. This is due to their uncompromisable focus and their attention and their thirst for knowledge.

Additionally, people with this personality have knowledge in any field or topic they focus on and contribute significantly to the subject. Categorically, an investigator can be very successful at self-development because of their zeal and aspiration for knowledge. They also like esoteric knowledge and can do very well if they devote themselves to the object of study and investigation. They are often seen as being withdrawn to their thoughts. Most of them are usually drawn to humanity, and it is not uncommon for them to have altruistic inclinations.

Investigators are usually drawn to their own thoughts because they get into a state of melancholy quickly. This makes them observe and research into the world without accepting the opinions of others. These kinds of people tend to be shy, non-intrusive, independent, and reluctant to ask for help even if others are happy to help them. They are quite sensitive and do not feel adequately defended against the world. To compensate for their sensitivity, they adopt the attitude of reckless indifference or intellectual arrogance, which has the unfortunate consequence of creating distance between them and others. However, as they are shy and sometimes antisocial, if they attempt to be social, they are often dedicated to friends and companions.

Intrinsically, you can hardly know what is going on in the emotions of these kinds of people because they often have stronger feelings than the one they express. They have the dire need for privacy, and this goes a long way in their social inclinations. They also fear that they do not have enough inner strength to face life, so they tend to withdraw and retreat into themselves. They feel more comfortable at home and in their realm of thought. A person of this personality has been identified by scholars of the Enneagram to face the challenges of eccentricity.

The fifth personality has a way of deviating from the usual norm. They are mental types who focus on intellectual understanding and accumulating knowledge. They are described as scholars because of their keen perception and analytical ability. However, the truth about the relentless seeking of knowledge is in response to insecurities about themselves. Their characteristics include being: analytical, thoughtful, unobtrusive, detached, privacy-seeking, self-sufficiency.

They have the following strengths: self-dependence, confidence in their own knowledge, observant, simplicity. However, the fifth character of the Enneagram also has the underlying fear of being incompetent and helpless. They fear that when they do not do what they like to do well, they are inadequate. Because of this underlying fear, they tend to be very analytic and conservative in their thoughts. Also, their desire for knowledge and mastery allows them to be indifferent and objective.

Challenges of the fifth personality of the Enneagram

Indifference

A person of this personality is usually also described as being apathetic or passive. They have been discovered to be void of feelings. They have no preference, and often seem biased in the way they relate to things. Practically, they are described as being impartial with no care and concern about different things in the world, and this is because they fear they lack the inner resources to cope with life.

The fundamental reason for their indifference is because of the way they think about the world, which is entirely different from the way others think about it. They tend to question the opinion of others and how things come into place, which makes them weird.

Withdrawal from others

Investigators, as stated earlier, are known to be withdrawn from the rest of the world. To put it simply, they are the shy type and are unable to open up to anything that can threaten their peaceful world even if it is their own emotions. They are not comfortable with dealing with the demand for relationships or competing for a place in the world, but once they are in a relationship with you, they tend to be dedicated. The primary reason they withdraw from others is that they enjoy privacy and being alone. Being alone allows them to revel in their own thoughts.

Intellectual Arrogance

Categorically, investigators are known to have academic brilliance. This is because after they question the existence of things in their mind, they do more by getting more information on the topic. To them, this means the opinion of others does not count anymore on the subject. They have more knowledge, and it is the basis on which they live. They love confinement, which allows them their own space to ruminate.

Eccentricity

The enneagram scholars describe people of this personality as eccentric because they possess the ability to deviate from the norm. They are not social but socially inclined in their thoughts. It should be noted that their thoughts allow them to be the way they are described.

Fears intrusion

The investigators fear that they might be intruded upon and therefore values privacy and mostly want to be alone. They are not-intrusive and are independent. Because they do not like to impose, they do not ask help from people even if people are willing to assist them. They love confinement and set boundaries for themselves.

Investigators can overcome their challenges and the adverse effects if they maintain and develop themselves in the following ways:

Creation and establishment of boundaries:

People of this kind of personality can set limits for others around them to avoid them invading their privacy. It should be noted that one of the challenges of the fifth personality is their fear of intrusion; therefore, the solution to this problem is the creation of boundaries.

Engage others:

The popular cliché 'no one is an island of knowledge' applies to the fifth personality of the Enneagram. In engaging others in their thoughts and emotions, a relationship is formed, and the ideas of others are also taken into consideration. It can also expand the available inner resources of people of this personality. This can solve one of the challenges of people of this personality, which is their intellectual arrogance.

Be with people:

Because of the kind of trait, the fifth personality possesses, they tend to restrain themselves to their own thoughts. The best they can do for themselves is to be in an environment where they can communicate vastly with people, and this enlightens explicitly and gives more knowledge about the world. As popularly said, 'energy is symbiotic,' connecting with the right form of energy makes people of the fifth personality expand their own life. The best people of the fifth personality of the Enneagram can do for themselves is to learn more with people rather than learning alone.

To conclude, the above solutions given to the fifth personality should be taken into considerations as it helps to maintain their thinking and improves the social life of people of this personality. It also helps them in becoming better; they could be the best of all the personality types if they take into consideration the above solutions. It would help them become better people, and also sharing the knowledge they get, assists people of other personalities.

Investigators are mostly highly successful scholars, investors, and entrepreneurs. They view the world on a whole other level and try their possible best to influence or even change it to their preference. A perfect example is Isaac Newton, Albert Einstein, and so much more. Now, don't let this get to your head.

Because your personality traits are related to these great men shouldn't be the premise for you to start feeling superior. Remember, the goal of this book is to keep you abreast with your personality and the personality of others for a healthy relationship and a prosperous world altogether. The sixth personality promises to be as exciting as this one. Thus, you don't want to miss it.

Chapter Ten
The Sixth Personality

The sixth personality type of the Enneagram is the Loyalist. Also known as the Skeptic or Loyal, the sixth personality is given its name because they are loyal to those close to them as well as their beliefs. Compared to the other types, loyalists tend to have longer-lasting relationships, sticking with people through thick and thin. They have an abundance of commitment and are all about security. Because of their tendency to keep their relationships, they are very reliable and trustworthy.

The description of Loyalists

People of the sixth personality are completely devoted. People, ideas, systems, doctrine; whatever they choose to be bonded to, they bond to, regardless of what might be against the adherence. Sometimes their beliefs do not necessarily align with those already laid down and hence might seem a little rebellious; however, this won't stop them from pushing limits for those beliefs.

Loyalists fight more for their beliefs than for themselves. They would also fight for anyone they feel stands up for those beliefs. This quality makes them amazing friends, and as long as the other party keeps showing support, they too will remain loyal to the end.

The primary reason for their unwavering loyalty to others is that they fear abandonment. They have little confidence in their own singular abilities and would prefer to have continuous support. This lack of faith doesn't necessarily mean that they never think about making decisions. Quite the contrary, they do - and they do it a lot. They do a lot of worrying about making decisions; hence, the need to be supported.

Despite the search for support, they try to avoid letting others make important decisions and forcing it on them. They like to feel supported/assisted and not controlled. While they are afraid of others forcing decisions on them, they still wouldn't want anything that puts them at the battlefront. They have second thoughts about some things, if not all things and find it hard to decide, especially when those decisions will have an effect on a lot more things and people than them.

They are always trying to build walls against their insecurity. They have so many things that make them feel anxious, and so they look for ways to lock those anxieties out, including finding solace in the many friends that they're loyal to. When they feel the walls will hold, and their friends will stand for them, their level of confidence will increase, and they will be more willing to take part more in decision-making activities.

As soon as they feel their level of support depleting in any way, their self-doubt and anxieties creep back in. When on their own, they are always in a struggle to find a way to stand on their own but finding that stance can turn them into some of the most courageous people.

People of the sixth personality tend to get attached. Their attachment is not only to people but also to ideologies and doctrines that they think to give them most strength. They require a feeling of solidity in their lives. Continually fearing that situations change makes them stick with the beliefs as something to always guide and support them when at a loss of human guidance. When they achieve a sense of stability -which they tend to find hard to do- they do not question it and would prefer that others do not as well. Once they achieve trust in others, they would move heaven and earth to make sure that the connection is maintained with the person. Such people might be in the position of a role model, teacher or close friend — anyone they can see as a paragon in whatever field.

Although it's been said that they are hesitant, people of the sixth personality can also be strong, aggressive, and defendant about what they believe in. A need to prove their loyalty can make them very courageous and forward. They are committed, reliable and due to their constant criticism of everything, they foresee problems and hence help prevent or solve them.

There are many well-known people of this personality including Mark Twain, Robert F. Kennedy, Malcolm X, George H. W. Bush,

Prince Harry, Mike Tyson, Eminem, Marilyn Monroe, Woody Allen, Julia Roberts, Jennifer Aniston, Ben Affleck, and Ellen Degeneres.

Challenges of the sixth personality of the Enneagram

Lack of Self Confidence

People of the sixth personality have very little faith in their prowess or ability. They also belittle their own judgment, conclusions, and convictions. This is why they rely so much on others and beliefs and need external support. They fear that being made to do or decide things will lead to total disaster. However, when these people have any form of stance, they continuously work on making their abilities known. They try to ensure that they receive credit for their hard work.

Being alone

Without any help or guidance, people of the sixth personality mostly float around indecisively and will find it hard to get anything at all done. If they do get things done, they spend a lot of time criticizing and belittling what they have done. Loyalists refuse to believe anything they do on their own would be enough and instead live by the phrase 'strength in numbers.' But when they feel supported or, are convinced of their abilities after a lot of critiquing, their fight changes from that of a need for support to a need to prove themselves.

Need to avoid confrontations

They do not like when they are told they aren't good enough or haven't done enough or that their ideas are worthless. They already do enough by doubting themselves and do not need anymore. Loyalists fear people finding faults in what they do or their thoughts, so they like to know they have back up and do constant self-evaluation making sure they find errors and solutions in those faults before anyone else does.

Overthinking

When they do things on their own, they always fear that they won't do well. Overthinking and constant critiquing and re-evaluation of themselves, their activities and thoughts is the only way they believe they can find faults before anyone else does. Their brains work overtime in hopes that they will encounter problems before anyone else might notice. When making decisions, they have a lot of second thoughts and would prefer to know that there's some form of back up. The overtime working their brains to make them excellent troubleshooters but deprives them of peace and a feeling of security.

Overachieving

They tend to want to do more than they can. This is mostly because they think the world expects a lot more from them than they can give. Rather than stick to what they can do with ease, they would rather believe that all they've done is way too little. They give their all while thinking there's more to be done.

Attachment

When they find people or ideologies that they believe make them stand firm and provide enough support, they risk getting attached. They would go to great lengths to ensure they keep these connections and beliefs and uphold them no matter what they might be risking. Sometimes, they eventually find it hard if they have to do anything without support from these people or beliefs which make them unable to achieve things on their own. They become very dependent and guarded when approached about it.

Insecurity

The feeling that there is nothing that'll remain sturdy for them to hold on to is a battle that Loyalists face all the time. Their vulnerability manifests in various forms such as anxiety, withdrawal, antisocial behavior, and avoiding leadership roles. Trust is hard for them, and they would rather be on their own, avoiding friendships and spontaneous activities. Loyalists would never delve into anything if they haven't thought and had second thoughts about it first.

It's not like they are boring, but the fear that something might go wrong at any time with anything rules them and makes them retreat from situations and things they have little or no knowledge about. When they are convinced and develop a sense of security, they begin to come out and take more chances if they feel supported. When a person proves supportive of them, they feel safe and develop this sense of courage that would make them go the extra mile for that person.

There you have it. In case you find yourself in this particular type of personality trait, then you now know the challenges you might likely face with time. Therefore, allowing you to find and create surprising ways to cross over these obstacles and become a better version of yourself. Be that as it may, being a loyalist is not such a bad idea after all.

Chapter Eleven
The Seventh Personality

In the previous chapter, we looked into the loyalist personality trait, its description, and its challenges. This chapter would focus on the seventh personality trait, which is called the enthusiast. The people with this personality are known for being outgoing, optimistic, adventurous, and often busy.

Enthusiasts are always looking for the next exciting thing and are often found engaging in any new activity they find. In short, they are always doing something. Enthusiasts are given the name enthusiast because of their level of enthusiasm toward new adventures. They have little consideration for whether or not they'll regret engaging in whatever it is they choose to but would instead look forward to it with much enthusiasm.

The description of the enthusiast

Do you possess this personality? Have you laid bare that foundation of which personality you belong? If you have and you find yourself getting aligned with the Enthusiast personality, then the first question that would most likely come to your mind is the description of this personality. Well, here it is. The enthusiast can't wait to get their hands into whatever is going on. Whatever that might seem exciting even if it's not necessarily worthwhile.

They welcome new tasks and look forward to finding more to do. People who fall into this category live like the whole world is an amusement park with lots of rides and they would try all if they could. Like children, the thought of new activities excites them, and they would pretty much do anything for this excitement. They fear negativity and people telling them they can't or shouldn't do those things that bring them excitement, so they often distract themselves by multitasking and engaging in things that they feel bring excitement. They focus on their strengths and abilities, so they can ignore all the areas they're lagging.

Always occupied either with the search for the next intriguing thing or doing something new. People of other personality traits tend to find people of the seventh personality somewhat undisciplined, unorganized, or scattered. The brain of enthusiasts tends to work overtime, though not exactly in an academic manner. However, they are quite knowledgeable with their thoughts ranging from one thing to another. They are very verbal and impulsive - wanting to act immediately on their thoughts and ideas- and it's all because they have so much they think they need to do.

Enthusiasts can be viewed as childlike due to the way they look for excitement in the littlest of things. They can delve into a singular idea and break it down into so many individual parts and find interest in all those different parts. Being able to pick out interest in the plainest of things is very admirable of people of the seventh personality.

When forced to do nothing or the minimal is when an enthusiast is most uncomfortable. Their minds reel and they are constantly reminded of all the other things they could and probably should be doing while they're stuck. To an Enthusiast, doing the minimum is a horror, and they would mostly prefer multitasking.

Juggling multiple jobs successfully no matter how tasking it may seem to others, is something that might come easy to them because they're always thinking of what to do next and the multiple jobs keep them occupied. Ensuring they live their life to the fullest, making memories and finding joy in the little things is the culture of Enthusiasts. If it interests them, spiking even the smallest amount of excitement in them, they go for it if they can. They enjoy and prefer the practical aspect rather than the theoretical and so they experiment a lot. Their excitement and enthusiasm are often very contagious and convincing to those who they come across. They know how to promote themselves, abilities and activities and how to convince people to buy into their ideas. This makes them trendsetters.

Because they continuously search for fun or the next big thing, they are often seen as 'the life of the party.' By continually looking for new ways to explore and unique things to do, they tend to be inventive, innovative, quick thinkers, and creative. Dabbling into a variety of things makes them multitalented, oriented, and restless. When they can hone these abilities, they end up very successful.

Examples of well-known people of personality seven are Galileo Galilei, W.A. Mozart, Thomas Jefferson, Benjamin Franklin, John F. Kennedy, Malcolm Forbes, Ted Turner, Elton John, Mick Jagger, Fergie, Miley Cyrus, Britney Spears, Katy Perry, Russell Brand, George Clooney, Brad Pitt, Jim Carrey, Mike Myers, Bruce Willis, Robert Downey Jr., James Franco, Leonardo DiCaprio, Cameron Diaz, Paris Hilton, and Simon Cowell.

Problems the seventh personality faces

Impulsiveness

Members of this personality category like to act on their initial instinct. They generally do the first thing that comes to mind or seems like would be most exciting without weighing the costs, risks, consequences, or the aftermath of what they get themselves into. This might make them come off as selfish, but they would instead go ahead on those adventures and address everything else later.

It also makes them seem rash, but quite the contrary; they're very thoughtful and intelligent. The ability of their brains to consider so many ideas and break down those ideas in a search for excitement proves that their minds work wonderfully and they are creative. Working mostly without plans and concerns for the future, they would rather live in the present and revel at the moment.

Life is an adventure that they must go on regardless of what the cost is. This impulsiveness is also their way to avoid dealing with negativity and the opinions of others. If they just work on things as it comes to mind, they wouldn't have to deal with what people have to say.

Being disorganized

By thinking of so much at once, wanting to juggle multiple activities and doing things without a plan, they seem disorganized. They might have a list of lots of things to do but would do those things as it comes to mind rather than putting it in a schedule or a particular order that can be followed. Because of this they often seem incompetent in the many jobs they juggle, but in actuality, it helps them get a lot more done because they go for the most tasking first and then onto the next one. Enthusiasts always have something going on and are always getting things done. Multitasking is one of their strengths, and they can focus on as many things as they want, which makes their disorganization an advantage to getting things done a lot faster.

Insufficient resources

Enthusiasts are continually thinking of the next form of exhilaration and how to get it but sometimes, they might not be buoyant enough in terms of money, or they may lack some other things needed to go on their latest adventure. Living life to the fullest can get a little hard when you always need things that you don't have and can't get to do it. If their first impulse is something that might seem unachievable because of resources - or rather, a lack of it, it affects people of the seventh personality, and they do not like feeling like they're being slowed down.

Confinement/Feeling Restricted

People of the seventh personality in their thinking and actions prefer when there are space and a variety of choices. Being held down in a particular place or in a specific time when there is so much more, they could be doing, and a lot more they could be thinking is something that comes off as disturbing to an enthusiast. A situation where they are held back from doing what they want is something an enthusiast would prefer to avoid.

If a particular activity doesn't give them as much excitement and they are thinking of a lot more they should be doing, they would instead ditch that activity and go for others hoping to find excitement in that.

The opinion of people telling them to slow down is also a form of restriction to them, so they avoid the negativity of these people.

Seeming inattentive

More often than not, those who fall into the enthusiast category are believed to be so busy that they have little or no time for others around them. This doesn't necessarily mean more excitement or adventure; people of the seventh personality barely pay attention to and instead focus more on how to pick a new interest. Things that seem to hold minimal interest are seen as trivial to people of the seventh personality, and they brush those things off quickly.

When someone else who expects enthusiasts to should know things that they didn't find interest in and they don't, the other person might find them inattentive or selfish, but in actuality, they are just so absorbed in the activities and finding excitement and pleasure rather than themselves.

Being enthusiastic over everything is not a crime. In fact, it is a good trait which would make you excel in life and your relationships. As an enthusiast, always focus on the brighter side of things, and everything would still fall into places even without lifting a finger. The next personality trait would be the challenger personality trait. Let's get to it, shall we?

Chapter Twelve
The Eighth Personality

The eighth, and second to last personality that we will look at in this book is called the challenger. They are named this because they never turn down challenges. It is more like they feed on these challenges. Challengers are quick to make decisions and have high confidence in the choices that they make. This confidence has earned them the nicknames of Willful, Powerful and Self-confident. They always feel the need to control the environment because of their surety. Because of this, they have also known for being quite dominating.

Characteristics of the Challenger

Influential and inspirational but sometimes becomes intimidating; people of the eighth personality do not like to show weakness. They would rather challenge those around them in order to show their resourcefulness and skill. They never miss a chance at turning a challenge into a means to better themselves. They make advances at taking control before anyone else has an opportunity even to try let alone acquiring any form of rule over them. They fear to be vulnerable and possibly being hurt or dominated by others.

There is no way around it challengers are highly competitive people. They will do anything to win and ensure that the perceived opponent has no advantage over them. They feel a need to win at everything, and revel in their strengths, abilities, and work. They not only dislike human control, but they also hate being controlled by circumstances. Much like the seventh personality we looked at, challengers do not like feeling restricted. Sometimes these two personalities are mistaken for one another. This is especially true when an eighth's dominant wing is a seven, or a seven's dominant wing is an eight.

No matter how much contradiction challengers face, they only want to do what seems right to them and would go to any length to achieve their goals. Unlike the seventh personality that goes to extremes in order to get what they want because of a need for excitement, challengers go to extremes because they want to prove their worth and show their strength. They don't mind being forced out of their comfort zones because they like the idea that they have the opportunity to give more than they usually do and be even better than they already are.

People who fit into the challenger category are both convincing and charismatic. Hence, they can be found in a variety of leadership positions. They tend to be the best in their different fields and can sometimes be seen as paragons of whatever it is they stand for. Because of their ability to exercise so much control and restraint, they significantly affect their society and believe they have a full understanding of how things should work. They expect that everyone follows them and will fight opposition at all costs. They also have powerful instincts that they'll follow at all costs rather than go along with someone else's or being convinced to ignore their instincts.

Much like people of the sixth personality, trust is not an easy thing to achieve for challengers, but when they do realize it, they make that person into a very close friend and give that person a level of importance in their lives. People of the eighth personality begin to use their protective instincts to defend these people who are close to them and would do anything to provide for those people.

Challengers do not appreciate any form of control over them. They fear allowing external factors to influence them and will fight no matter what to break that influence. They choose to always grow their power, resources, and skills, which puts them way ahead of any threats of being overthrown. They are the most independent of all the types of personalities of the Enneagram.

Challengers might listen to advice from others, but they ensure they have the final say. They like to make sure they and no one else is the decision maker in their lives. Because of this, they often have problems with hierarchy if they aren't at the top. They often come off as rebellious because they are so strong-willed and feel a need for their opinions to heard and acknowledged.

When it comes to fears and concerns, people of this personality fear physical harm. But their primary fear is the feeling of being vulnerable in any way. Sometimes, challengers find intimate relationships hard to participate in because it requires a level of vulnerability, and people of this personality do not like to open up. This, combined with a fear of betrayal, also makes it difficult for challengers to engage in intimate relationships with anyone. It's not like they are entirely unfeeling. They have sentimental sides but would rather keep those sites hidden so that no one can see them as vulnerable or see those sentiments as an opportunity to gain control over them.

People well known in their various fields or groups are most likely perfect examples of challengers. People such as Donald Trump, Queen Latifah, Serena Williams, Pablo Picasso, and Franklin Roosevelt, Ernest Hemingway, James Brown, Pink, Jack Black, and Humphrey Bogart all fit into this category.

Weaknesses of the Eighth Personality

Rigidity/ Stubbornness

People who fit this category tend to be stiff. They aren't quick to listen to advice, and if they do, they don't find it easy to work on it, especially when they have their own ideas and beliefs of how things should go. To them, their decisions, cultures, routines, and actions are always the best, and no other alternative is good enough for them. If eventually, they choose to change anything about their approach to life and anything else, it would take a lot of convincing, which can often take a lot of time and explanation.

This can affect decision-making processes sometimes, especially since they tend to be in leadership positions and barely ever make any room for others to have any form of influence over them, despite their need for improvement. No matter how much they seek improvement, if they aren't convinced that a particular way is the right way, they won't involve themselves in it and would keep on searching until they find some form of conviction from any other thing.

Pride

Since the challengers tend to end up in leadership positions, their lack of attention to ideas and opinions of others might make them come off as proud. With so much confidence in their decisions, skills, and resources, they pay minimal attention to those of others that are 'inferior' to them.

They live by the 'you can't please everyone' line, and so they don't care when others aren't in favor of decisions they've made or actions they've taken as long as it is the best decision to them. They would rather face opposition than try to get on everyone's good side by compromising on whatever it is that isn't completely accepted. They often need a lot of conviction before admitting that they are wrong or that someone else is better than they are in any way.

Intimidating

Challengers tend to carry themselves with such high esteem that those who feel very little confidence in themselves might end up intimidated by them. Sometimes, people of the eighth personality might not be doing this on purpose. In fact, they're usually too busy working on themselves and how to improve actually to notice those who don't feel adequate about themselves.

Their ability to keep going despite opposition without any apparent hint of being disturbed also adds to a challenger's aura of intimidation. They are so hell bent on improving themselves that it seems like nobody else matters unless it is those that they've achieved a level of intimacy and trust with.

Overworking

The fear that anyone can gain control over them or be seen as a better counterpart makes people of the eighth personality ever at work to prove they are the best and deserve the control. Challengers are always working on acquiring more skills and improving their already acquired skills. Despite all the confidence they have in their abilities they always feel 'I can be better' and hence, are always looking for ways to surpass whoever might seem like a threat to the position they hold and the control they wield.

Even with all these weaknesses, challenges are very valuable to society and groups because they provide a certain amount of drive and inspiration to do things in the very best way. With someone of the eighth personality, there's always a need to get better and surpass those around because of their level of competitiveness. Challengers believe they are, or can be the best and so expect nothing less from their groups. Now let's get to the last personality trait, shall we?

Chapter Thirteen
The Ninth Personality

The peacemaker or the Easygoing is the ninth personality of the Enneagram. They are quick to trust, comply, and see the bright side of things. They are simply known as the optimists or even idealists. This particular set of people never seize to see the good in every situation, no matter how dim it may turn out to be in the end. They are with the belief that there is always a better side to everything. If you find yourself in this category of people, then lucky you.

The Ninth Personality Characteristics

People of the ninth personality detest and try very hard to avoid and minimize conflict. They are wonderful troubleshooters since they strive for peace in every form; most especially inner peace. They are very accepting and will embrace everyone who wants to be in their lives, regardless of their flaws. Of all the nine personalities, they try the most to maintain peace. Peacemakers possess characteristics such as being friendly, adaptable, agreeable, and easygoing and a people pleaser.

Most people of the ninth personality always like a place that is chaos-free, and this is the primary reason why they might sometimes be introverted. They want to insulate themselves from the world that is free of problems. However, they are usually likable and steady and sometimes social and active in their dealings, but even their social life and a part of them is kept in reserve. They are more focused on blending in that they sometimes do not care about themselves.

The ninth personality of the Enneagram also exhibits the ability to become good parents because they are good listeners, and they are not judgmental. Although they do not like problems and they do not like the existence of problems, so they try as much as possible to retreat than face the problem.

The ninth personality of the Enneagram is also the most spiritual of all of them. Always trying to find balance in both worlds, Peacemakers enjoy when there is a connection and as little tension as possible. Despite their spirituality, people of the ninth personality can be deeply rooted in their physicality as well.

They tend to be more focused on their feelings. Their ability not to tolerate disorder or conflict translates into an approach for change. One of their other characteristics is their ability to adapt to change. Because of their urge for peacemaking, they are usually trustworthy and they lead a more active social media life to get them involved. Their peacemaking and mediating ability makes them tolerant of their environment. They also avoid negative emotions around them; they feel more secure with a secured environment with peace.

Basically, people who fit into this personality category detest being overlooked, and this is why they are notable for peacemaking and their participation cannot be ignored. However, people of the ninth personality often hate what will be a threat to their peace or the peace of their environment. They also mistake their own identities because they do not have much sense of it, and they have traits like a people pleaser, agreeable, adaptable, trusting, easygoing, and empathetic. The fact that they like to please people around them makes them forget their own dreams and emotions. Instead, they prefer focusing on the peace and calm of the environment.

They are usually very likable and open-minded because of their impact, and they generally have no hate in them and want everyone to get along. However, the primary reason why people of this personality are introverted is that they need to excuse themselves from a world of chaos. They are usually very relaxed and collected and out of touch from their emotions because they try to work on other people's feelings and the peace of their surroundings. They are good coordinators, and they always believe that things will work out fine and they are usually good friends. They give a friendly ear to every problem anybody around them has and are always very positive about situations around them.

They are always supportive and loving and will never judge the situation. However, they always find a solution to the problem and try to make peace. Also, people of this personality usually have a cooperative nature, and this is why they are friendly. However, this personality also has its own challenges because they do more selfless services without being reminded of themselves. The issues that people of this personality face include:

Stubbornness or rigidity

People of this personality are often rigid in their decision making. They always find it hard to let go of injustice. They are usually stubborn when they make decisions and could become violent when their opinions are not taken into consideration. Another reason for their stubborn trait is that, as their name implies, they are meant to make peace, but when they cannot make the peace they desire, they become stubborn and hard-hearted.

Low self-esteem

The ninth personality, although very friendly, can be a victim of low self-worth. This is because they feel there is a particular worth attached to them, and when they do not meet up to their worth, they will not be able to participate in their peacemaking activities.

Indecisiveness

Another major challenge of the ninth personality of the Enneagram is the problem of indecisiveness. Because of the ninth personality's love for peace and harmony, they tend to be sometimes indecisive, especially in the way they make decisions. They are the kind of people that always want everything that concerns them to go on smoothly.

Ambivalence

The challenge of uncertainty is also an issue for this personality. This challenge can also relate to the challenge of indecisiveness. A person of the ninth personality seems to change opinions as they like. Their views usually alternate, and this might not make them perform their peacemaking activity well.

Forgetfulness

This is also a significant challenge people of the ninth personality face. This challenge can equally relate to the problems above. Because they are indecisive and cannot make a decision, they even tend to forget their recent decision and go for the latter. Although they love peace and are usually cooperative and agreeable, they do not become good leaders, but they are rather good followers in any field they delve into.

These challenges are often as a result of the fact that they are more people willed than self-willed. Peacemakers are also described as conflict avoidant can overcome the problems above and motivate themselves in the following ways:

Internal Peace

Peacemakers should note that their own internal environment needs to be maintained before the external harmony of the situation. There is a need for conflict avoidant to value themselves first and recognize that they will be forefront in the peacemaking.

Desire happiness

A ninth personality person also deserves to be happy instead of trying to always blend in with the world. They should be able to think about their own happiness instead of being bothered about the chaos around them and the way to settle it.

Overcoming conflict

It is essential that peacemakers need to understand that not all disputes can be engaged in, and there could be peace in chaos. There is always a way to avoid getting into every conflict, although as peacemakers, they need to avoid it even when the conflict can't be avoided, it can be overcome.

Believe in yourself

There is also the need for people of the ninth personality to love themselves and do what they want. They need to believe in themselves, especially when making decisions that might affect them. They need to understand that their needs, desires, and emotions are as important as everyone else's.

To conclude, although the ninth personality do not make good leaders, they are usually good with whatever they do if they put their mind to it and put themselves and their happiness first.

Chapter Fourteen
The Instinctual Variants of Enneagram

In the Enneagram, three centers of intelligence are described - one of which is the Body/instinctual Centre. The body center has three instinctual drives, all of which we use during our day to day activities, but, one, in particular, is most important to different people and influences the expression of personality type.

Everyone has all three instinctual variants at work in their lives, but there is a major one that governs their life and how they live it. It's easier to figure out which subtype is the major governor (primary subtype) for some people, while for others; it takes a lot of time and study. Sometimes people derive information from the opinions of people about them because it can be tricky to see ourselves in the right light and not the light we want to see.

For all of the nine Enneagram types, there are variations of these three subtypes giving a total of twenty-seven. The subtypes explain what is most important to an individual. What we focus on and provide maximum attention to is determined by these subtypes. A person would most likely identify with all of the subtypes in their Enneagram, but it's essential to know which one has more control. Based on the subtypes, an individual has tendencies and potential to excel in certain areas of their instinctual lives.

The three Instinctual Variants/ Subtypes are:

The Self Preservation Instinct

This deals with oneself. It controls us; as we strive for survival. This instinctual variant determines a person's basic needs for survival, such as shelter, food, security, and all related. People focused on this instinctual variant focus more on endurance and basic needs concerned with it. They prioritize comfort and safety.

Arrangement, neatness, cleanliness, temperature, and even the status of their fridge and groceries all matter to them. Concerning their food, they either have a lot because they indulge or very little because they're on strict diets. They are very practical when it comes to taking care of all the basic life necessities such as bills and getting provisions. They also try very hard to be independent and pay little or no attention to relationships and interactions with others. They show a lower level of spontaneity compared to those of the other instinctual variants.

For this Instinctual variant, the nine are:

>Personality 1, The Perfectionist: Anxiety (The Pioneer)

>Personality 2, The Giver: Privilege (The Nurturer)

>Personality 3, The Performer: Security (The Company man/woman)

>Personality 4, The Romantic: Dauntlessness (The Creative Individualist)

>Personality 5, The Observer: Home (The Castle Defender)

>Personality 6, The Loyalist: Warmth (The Family Loyalist)

>Personality 7, The Enthusiast: Family (The Gourmand)

>Personality 8, The Challenger: Satisfactory Survival (The Survivalist)

>Personality 9, The Peacemaker: Appetite (The Collector)

The Sexual Instinct

This deals with personal interaction with other individuals. It controls all form of relationships with others such as sexuality, closeness with friends, and intimacy. Because of the name, a lot of people think the intimate relationships refer only to sexual attraction, but it is a lot more than that for people of this instinctual variant. They appreciate and crave the intensity of their one-on-one relationship with the people they choose.

Unlike the people of the instinctual social variant, people who are focused on the sexual instinct prefer one on one relationships with people, rather than the whole deal of social interactions and activities with large groups. When captivated by people, they have tendencies of ignoring all other matters even if they seem pressing to spend a lot more time with whoever has their attention. They can seem promiscuous because of the focus to every person who captures their attention in any way, but they do not always manifest in the form of sexuality. Their relationships are incredibly important to them. They are very passionate compared to the three other instinctual variants and put more energy into the one on one relationships they have.

The nine are:

> Personality 1, The Perfectionist: Jealousy/Zealousness (The Evangelist)
>
> Personality 2, The Giver: Seduction/Aggression (The Lover)
>
> Personality 3, The Performer: Femininity/Masculinity (The Movie Star)
>
> Personality 4, The Romantic: Competitiveness (The Dramatic Person)
>
> Personality 5, The Observer: Confidentiality (The Secret Agent)
>
> Personality 6, The Loyalist: Strength/Beauty (The Warrior)
>
> Personality 7, The Enthusiast: Suggestibility/Fascination (The Adventurer)
>
> Personality 8, The Challenger: Possession /Surrender (The Commander)
>
> Personality 9, The Peacemaker: Union (The Seeker)

Social Instinct

This involves dealing with groups. This instinctual variant determines a person's need to fit into society. The concerns of people focused on this instinctual variant are mostly concerned with social activities and their relation with other members of their community. They tend to be active members of clubs, groups, parties, and any other form of socialization. They derive a sense of value or esteem from participating in social activities such as work, family, social gatherings, and many more.

Their sense of belonging usually serves as a form of safety for them. They enjoy social interactions but avoid intimacy. They like to know what is going on and be filled in when it comes to trends and in-things, making them quick to jump on trends and socially active and knowledgeable. They focus on interactions that would build their social status and belong in society.

The nine are:

Personality 1, The Perfectionist: In-adaptability (the Social Reformer)

Personality 2, The Giver: Ambition (The Ambassador)

Personality 3, The Performer: Prestige (The Politician)

Personality 4, The Romantic: Shame/Honor (The Critical Commentator)

Personality 5, The Observer: Totem Symbols (The Professor)

Personality 6, The Loyalist: Duty (The Social Guardian)

Personality 7, The Enthusiast: Limitation/Sacrifice (The Utopian Visionary)

Personality 8, The Challenger: Friendship/Social Causes (The Group Leader/Gang Leader)

Personality 9, The PeaceMaker: Participation (The Community Benefactor)

Understanding exactly where you fall is of importance as that is the only way you can become the best version of yourself as well as influencing the lives of the people around you for the better. Each center of intelligence holds unique and specific qualities, thus, forcing oneself to be what he or she is not would be highly disadvantageous in the long run. Therefore, if you have found your path, then I will suggest you stick to it.

Chapter Fifteen
The Enneagram and Social Relations

This is obviously the chapter you are really interested in before picking this book. I'm sure you must have been puzzled by the question of how to really interact with the people around you without going into unnecessary headlocks and tiffs. This is what this chapter will delve into. All thanks to Enneagram, all your relationships and connections will stay in shape. Nevertheless, how does Enneagram ensures a successful relationship? Let's find out.

As social beings, it is impossible for humans to be on their own. Every day, we come in contact with various people of various personalities, and it can get tricky dealing with things like that. There are misunderstandings, challenges, and situations where it seems impossible to deal with these people.

This is because people come in any of the nine personalities of the Enneagram and others even switch between personalities. Even those that are of the same Enneagram personality as ourselves might not be of the same subtypes. Dealing with others around us becomes a task, and since everyone has the instinct of self-preservation, which can make us selfish, we would rather not put in the effort.

Through the insight that Enneagram gives into a person and those around that person, making better relationships with all those around us is made a lot easier. When a person understands another person's view of the world, it helps create empathy, compassion, and appreciation of that person's views.

Understanding the different Enneagram types equips us with the tools needed in starting and maintaining proper relationships with whomever and in whatever form. We learn how to work together, even when faced with opposition and avoid conflicts. By understanding each Enneagram type, our eyes are open to the desires, fears, and concerns of people of the various Enneagram types; hence, our relationships are improved automatically.

No matter how long we've known certain people and where we come across new people, making an effort to understand their enneagram types will save us from a lot of conflict and misunderstanding. Being in a situation where you have no idea what people are like and how to address and deal with them can make a ruckus out of what should be productive or fun.

Everyone wanting to do things differently, and no one understanding why or even trying to compromise will take all form of effectiveness away from the purpose of the gathering. It takes someone who studies people around them and understands their personalities to know how to derive productivity from socializing.

A person with a proper understanding of the Enneagram will be more confident about meeting people and making appropriate connections. They'll worry less about not doing enough or doing too much because they know exactly where to draw the line after a little time spent with the other party. Communication becomes key, and if issues do occur, they know what to do to minimize and eventually solve them. They also have longer lasting relationships that are built on understanding despite differences in behavior, outlook, and reactions.

Our social relations are also affected by the subtypes of the instinctual social variants of our Enneagram personalities. The instinctual social option has a lot to do with our need for belonging in society. For people who are focused in this instinctual variant, their roles, status, and personalities in society matter a lot more than close relationships to individuals and themselves.

Personality 1, The Perfectionist

In-adaptability(the Social Reformer)

Due to their need to do things the right way, people of this subtype find it hard to adapt to changes in society, and situations and might even lead to the criticizing of those that stray from the laid down rules, methods, and approaches of doing things in society. They do not appreciate changes in how society is run; hence the name 'in-adaptability'. They try to ensure that society runs smoothly with a defined set of rules.

Personality 2, The Giver: Ambition (The Ambassador)

These people search for social approval, a feeling of being indispensable and being a highly representative member of society. Despite all this, they put more importance in relating with the right people than actually being head of the group.

Personality 3, The Performer: Prestige (The Politician)

People of this subtype aim toward social power. They enjoy influencing society in any way, including the government which they achieve by working on their social image.

Personality 4, The Romantic: Shame/Honor (The Critical Commentator)

These people tend to feel smaller compared to those of high status in society and chase status of their own. In need to achieve an acceptable role in society, they can be the most honest of people. They sometimes harbor envy toward those that have the roles they crave.

Personality 5, The Observer: Totem Symbols (The Professor)

People of this subtype seek knowledge and like to observe and learn from society and its communication systems. Because of all their attention to how society works, sometimes, they get stuck just observing society rather than being active members.

Personality 6, The Loyalist: Duty (The Social Guardian)

In a need to belong, these people learn and live out the rules ensuring they are on the right terms with members of society. They also seek out the rules like 'The Professor,' but it's for clarity. So that they know they are acting right in society.

Personality 7, The Enthusiast: Limitation/Sacrifice (The Utopian Visionary)

Their love of life and enjoyment of certain social activities makes people of this subtype at a need for friends. Meanwhile, this socialization sometimes is a burden to them as it leaves them with less opportunity to expand themselves the way they please.

Personality 8, The Challenger: Friendship/Social Causes (The Group Leader/Gang Leader)

These people are quick at finding leadership roles in society. They harness their aggression into fuel for the group.

Personality 9, The Peacemaker: Participation (The Community Benefactor)

Their selflessness makes them beautiful candidates for leadership positions in society although it always leaves them with less time and attention for themselves.

Nothing beats having a smooth relationship with the people around you. No one can live in a complete state of autarky even if they plan to. We all must relate with one another at any point in time. Now, how do we make this easy, smooth, and successful relationship happen? You guessed it – Enneagram. Know yourself, know the people around you, and every other thing will just fall into place.

Chapter Sixteen
The Enneagram and Parenting

I'm sure that we can all agree that raising children is an entirely mind-boggling and at times, overwhelming experience. More often than not, the personality of children differs significantly from that of their parents, which makes understanding and knowing how to treat them properly becomes a hard task. A lot of times, parents try so hard to understand their children; thinking it holds all the answers when in actuality, they should put more effort into understanding themselves.

Enneagram assists people in parenting by teaching them about their personalities in relation to those of their children. When the parent has proper knowledge of who he/she is, how he/she behaves and his/her approach to their children and their upbringing, it makes parenting a less tasking job than it seems. While it is beneficial, the Enneagram should not be used by parents as a way to describe or act to towards their kids because their personality might change as they grow up.

While understanding one's personality in relation to parenting, the personalities of the children as well should not be left out. When Children's personalities are understood as much as that of their parents, it teaches how the children are to be approached their likes and dislikes, fears, and desires. Knowledge of the Enneagram also helps us understand how the parent and child can relate best based on their types.

Through proper understanding of the Enneagram, a lot of "I don't know" and "Why don't you understand why I'm doing this?" that arise can be avoided. Parents can predict their child's actions, wants, and reactions in certain situations. Children evolve and change, and in the process of interacting with them the different personalities in them come out because they exhibit multiple characters, primarily because of their parents. A proper understanding of a child's Enneagram personality and that of the parent in relation to it will help build better relationships between the two and help avoid conflicts that might have happened because of their differences.

When a parent knows what his/her child's Enneagram personality is, the parent can quickly determine how to make that child happy, what makes the child feel inadequate or threatened, and where to make compromises so the child can grow in the most proper and positive way possible. There is no peace between two people of different personalities if there is no communication, understanding, and compromise. Extensive knowledge of personalities explains a lot about how to communicate correctly in the most effective ways.

Sometimes, a person's regular personality might differ from their parenting personality. Their normal personalities remain but can change when dealing with children. Someone who is typically a Peacemaker (the ninth personality) might become a Challenger (the eighth personality) when dealing with children probably because they feel a need to have control over their children or some other reason. Whatever the reason is and whatever the change is, knowledge of the Enneagram will give the needed confidence, conviction, and understanding for dealing with the children.

However, no parent is perfect, and while knowing the Enneagram or personality of your child can help to raise them into successful adults and make them understand their own personality as well and improve on themselves parents are still going to face challenges along the way. It is essential that parents should create an avenue for their children to discover their personality or Enneagram. It should be noted that the personality types are in different groups and will be identified below with the way the parents can connect with their personality.

The Confident Type:

The Third Personality (The Achievers)

Children of the third personality are usually very energetic, and they always want to take charge and be active in their environment, and they always like to keep themselves busy. They also like to show themselves and not only do they need to achieve as their name implies, they like to be at the forefront in everything they do; in other words, they want to showcase themselves.

Parenting children of this personality type is not as difficult as it might seem. Although parenting is not an easy job; parents of kids with this personality really have to encourage their children and boost their morale. It is also essential that they advise them to slow down in competing with others. Parents should also note that the reassurance of their unconditional love for their children also helps the children and the creation of a better environment also helps the children.

The Seventh Personality (The Enthusiasts)

The characteristic of this category of people has been stated earlier, and these characteristics are also peculiar to children of this personality as well. However, children in this category are full of life, and they can get bored quickly. They are usually not concerned about the fun of others as long as they are having fun. They always make sure they divert their attention from boredom, and they always make things interesting for themselves. Parents of children of this personality can help their children by participating in the fun activities and adventure of their children.

The Eighth Personality (The Challenger)

Children of this category are usually outspoken and never afraid to express their opinions. They become aggressive if they are unable to express their views. They are generally full of energy, and they always try to help others. Parenting this category of children requires a lot of effort, and parents have to keep a close watch on their children. Parents need to set boundaries if their children are of this personality type, and they need to give their children reasons for setting those boundaries; thereby, they keep a close watch on their children.

The Shy or Withdrawn Type

The Fourth Personality (The Individualists)

Parents of children of this personality can help them by nurturing their creativity because they seem to be very individualistic. They have a problem expressing their emotions. Because of this, parents should create an avenue for them to express their feelings. Parents should help their children if they are part of this personality type to get rid of bad energy around them.

The Fifth Personality (The Investigators)

Generally, people of this personality are majorly withdrawn and like to keep to themselves. However, they possess academic brilliance, and they love books. They question the existence of things in their mind, and they can be helped to encourage them and make them realize that their thoughts and emotions matter on essential matters. They should best be engaged in fun activities, games and anything and everything that will keep them in confinement.

The Ninth Personality (The Peacemakers)

The peacemakers are an exceptional kind, and they always make sure that there is peace in the family. They always do well by making sure that there is no conflict in their environment. It should be noted that parents of children of this personality must make their children accept the fact that it is not only their responsibility to keep the peace of the family, but it also requires everyone's efforts.

The Dutiful or Obedient

The First Personality (The Reformer)

This category of children loves to do the right thing at all times, and love to please and satisfy everybody around them. This category of children needs to be assured that it is fine not to get everything right. Their opinions should be respected especially when they give themselves more responsibility or feel a sense of duty in making it a better place.

The Second personality (The helper)

These children want to be loved and accepted the way they are. They love to help others and are in a way similar in personality with children of the first personality. They need to feel loved at all times, and they need to understand that self-care is vital in taking of others.

Parents of these children must pay attention to their needs and emotions.

The Sixth Personality (The Loyalists)

The young loyalist is concerned with the safety and security of other members of the family. At a point, they fear they might lose their family, and they feel it is their responsibility to keep the others safe. Their parents can help them by assuring them of safety so that their fear and anxiety may cease. They also need to discover their inner strength, and their need for security must be honored.

The incidence of different personalities in situations like these is why a person needs to go beyond a child's own personality. Rather, one should have a decent amount of knowledge on all of the other personalities in the Enneagram. It is important to realize that the more you know, the better you are at handling whatever kind of personality traits your children have.

It is also important to remember that as a child grows, their personality might change over time possibly more than once but knowing how to handle all of the different personalities will give the parent an edge over whatever challenges that they will have to face. However, the above-listed way of connecting and parenting children with different personalities should be well taken into consideration, and it should not be made a criterion in caring for their children.

Are you a parent or aspiring to be one? If you are one, then I'm pretty sure you have an idea of the massive churn of responsibilities that comes with being a parent. And if you aren't, then I will leave that to your imagination. However, being a parent is not an easy job. It takes the grace of God for one to be able to hold it together. Thus, why struggle with parenting when Enneagram could make it easier for you. Enneagram, if studied properly can make parenting become a much easier journey with everything turning out as great as you imagined.

Chapter Seventeen
The intelligence of Enneagram

There are three centers of intelligence, namely the head, the heart, and the gut. All three, although different, need to be accessed and be synchronized with each other. When life becomes harmonious when you derive knowledge from the three centers, but some personalities are more open to individual centers than others. The centers are more open to being their primary means of acting or react. The centers are typically useful for growth, and it should be noted that the centers of intelligence are essential in teaching and identifying the personality types.

In the aspect of development, the centers are a kind of the framework that helps to know how and why we are working with the Enneagram. The centers are also purposeful to being productive with our different systems and personalities. It is also useful for growth and requires a deepening of our relationship with all of the centers. However, it should be noted that the three centers of intelligence stated above could mean that we have three brains that work with our bodies system and relates to our personality. The three centers of intelligence can also be described as mental intelligence, heart intelligence, and body intelligence.

Ideally, we want to access all of the three centers, and that is why the three centers have their own functions. The head is responsible for thinking while the heart is the thinking arena, and the body or gut is instinctive. No matter what personality we possess, we have all of these three centers, and one cannot work without the other. There is a kind of an interaction between the three centers. In fact, the center that our personality works relates to our psyche that allows us to be able to perform freely. It is essential that we know the different centers we participate in according to our personality.

In the Centers of Intelligence, each enneagram personality has special names. They are;

Personality 1: Perfectionist

Personality 2: Giver

Personality 3: Performer

Personality 4: Tragic Romantic

Personality 5: Observer

Personality 6: Loyal Skeptic

Personality 7: Epicure

Personality 8: Protector

Personality 9: Mediator

The Head Centre:

Also called the thinking center consists of personality 5, 6, and 7. This center of intelligence allows us with the wisdom of the presence of information. However, when we lose presence, we lose the capacity or capability of this intelligence. The head center of knowledge has a common emotion, which is fear.

This center gives knowledge through reasoning, analyzing, imagining, and assessment. The personalities in this center enjoy the information and all its processes; hence, they can easily link ideas. The head center personality type wants security and is majorly concerned with strategies and beliefs.

They do not enjoy uncertainty. All the Enneagram personalities in this center have fear as their primary emotional issue. However, personality types with the head or thinking center of intelligence have various strengths and weaknesses depending on this center, and their weaknesses and strengths are stated below:

Weaknesses: *Strengths:*

The fifth personality;

- Being withdrawn
- Withholding
- The feeling of isolation.
-
-

Scholarly
thoughtful and dependable
intellectual & brilliant
respectful
perceptive

The sixth personality;

- Being negative
- Hyperactive
- Being opposite
- Imagination
- Hyperactive

Also perceptive
loyal and warm
courageous and funny
strategic thinking

The seventh personality;

- Arrogance
- Uncommitted
- Unrealistic
- Impatient

full of life
positive thinkers
playful
quick thinking

Each of the personalities under this center of intelligence has its own reaction to their major weakness and common emotion, which is fear. The fifth personality reacts to their emotional fear by distracting their minds, and most times, their surrounding affects the way they respond to the alarm. Personality six is usually prepared for the worse, and as such, they are already prepared for the emotional fear, and they typically seek guidance to deal with their inner self, which is afraid.

However, the seventh personality has a different way they react to fear. They try to make uncomfortable situations into comfortable situations because they fear they may be trapped in emotional pain. They always make sure their mind is occupied with something that will distract them.

The Heart Centre

The heart center or feeling center helps to know the truth of our personality and our identity. It is also a center that gives a sense of meaning to the value and glory of our existence. Personality types two, , and four usually use the heart center of intelligence. They always seek for recognition and validation, and this is because we do not have the capacity of self-reflection. The personality types under this center of intelligence always want attention, and when they do not get it, they feel shameful because they are more concerned with self-image.

Here, knowledge is through emotion, atmosphere, and feeling. The personalities do not enjoy rejection but can always identify what emotional qualities are best for specific situations and would get them accepted. The main emotional issue for the Enneagram personalities in this center is distress or shame. The weaknesses and strengths of the personalities of this center are as follows:

Weaknesses: *Strengths:*

The Second personality:

- Pride
- Demanding
- Intrusive
- Privileged

Generous and supportive
Sensitive to others feelings
helpful
loves relationship

The Third Personality:

- Competitive
- Impatient
- Overworked
- Image-driven

Successful
Efficient and practical
Competent and enthusiastic

The Fourth Personality:

- Mood swings
- Shy
- Self-absorbed
- Demanding
- Oversensitive

Creative
Opposite thinking
Compassion
Idealistic

Personalities of this center also have a way they react to their common emotion, which is distress or shame, and this is because they have a distortion in their feelings. People who fall into the second type of personality are usually caring, so they barely feel shame, and they also create an avenue of being likable and of reach when needed. The third personality, however, requires the approval of others on their accomplishment before they can cover up their shame. They usually seek the admiration of others. The last personality of this center which is the fourth personality react to their emotional distortion of shame by looking for a reason why they are unique, they create and sustain their moods, and they use their emotion as a way to defend rejection.

The Gut/Body Centre

This is where instinct and intuition come to play in knowledge. The personalities of this center make decisions based on instincts, and the personalities of this center of intelligence are personality types one, eight, and nine. They are sensual and feel more compassion compared than the others. They have strong opinions and tend to have just two views of every life situation. The Enneagram personalities' main emotional issue is anger, which comes from the instinctual response to the sense of feeling interference. This body center type is concerned with the control of the environment. Personalities within this center of intelligence also have their own strengths and weaknesses. They are:

Weaknesses: *Strengths:*

The Eighth Personality

- Anger and dominating   Courageous and truthful
- Fear of vulnerability   Determined and generous
- Excessive and lustful   Protective of others

The Ninth Personality

- Indecisive   Supporting others
- Peacemaking   Care about others
- Forgetfulness   Steady and adaptive
- Stubbornness

The First personality

- Judgmental
- Critical
- Hateful
- Rigid and bold

honest and trustworthy
accepts responsibility
hardworking and self-reliant

Personalities in this category also have a shared emotion, which is anger, and they react and control it in different ways. However, Personality eight of this center of intelligence respond to their anger by acting it out and never letting their guard down. Their anger usually arises due to injustice. The ninth personalities are usually disconnected with their anger, and they often find peace internally and externally. The last personality of this center of intelligence that is personality one and they do not like to express their inner anger. They like to repress their unconscious impulses.

In conclusion, If you find it hard determining what enneagram personality is yours, then finding out what your primary center of intelligence is can help narrow it down. If you're a logical and ever assessing person, then you're anyone of the personalities of the Head center (five, six or seven). An emotional person is any one of the Heart Triad (two, three or four). Although personality nine is one that always tries to appease others and resolve conflict and so acting like a member of the heart triad, this personality belongs to the body triad with personalities eight and one. Yearning for physical sensation and making decisions based on intuition, this triad is one that believes in instinct even when it might be wrong.

Chapter Eighteen
The Application of Enneagram

Being in the position to draw upon the knowledge of Enneagram, no matter how vast, matters minimally if it isn't correctly applied. With Enneagram, the combination of the three centers of intelligence that makes up a personality is appropriately put out in such a way that it can be applied in various settings. In profession, relationships, spirituality, and leisure understanding our Enneagram and that of others we come across are beneficial. The knowledge of the Enneagram must be put to good use in order to achieve maximum understanding and getting in touch with the environment.

Applying the knowledge we have about our Enneagram types makes it easier to express ourselves. It helps to know in detail what you prefer and how you like to be treated. Knowledge of our Enneagram types and living by that knowledge brings fulfillment to those who do it right. Identifying what might be a threat to your balance and what might offend you becomes more natural and can be controlled and put in check. By properly living based on your knowledge of your Enneagram personality, you get synchronized with yourself.

Your eyes are open to who you really are and how to live in that aspect. It's similar to having access into the inner workings of your own mind. Predicting your reactions to certain things and being able to tell what helps curb reactions that might throw you off, or that you might find to be wrong or outrageous - and you might regret after. Knowing about the wings of the Enneagram also helps you realize the suppressed parts of whom you are and when that part comes to play. Hence, a person lives a life of bliss and openness.

It's only typical that one first understands their own Enneagram personality type before anybody else's. After you find and comprehend your stance in the Enneagram personality types, then it's on to studying those around to know their place. Doing this is crucial because it helps build proper relationships and eradicates all that can stand as obstacles, challenges, issues, and misunderstandings.

Just being able to identify the personality type of those we come in to contact with on a daily basis is not enough but by applying conscious effort to make compromises and doing things to appease them, it can be said that you are correctly using the knowledge of Enneagram. When the majority of people are educated on enneagram types, and they make an effort to maintain peace and good relationships via this knowledge, then it can be said that Enneagram is being properly applied.

Whether or not you're able to quickly identify the enneagram type of others around matters very little; next to using the knowledge to make the most of these relationships. It might take a little dedication, but eventually, the understanding of a particular individual's Enneagram type will come easier to you. You tend to be slow to judge a person when you understand their Enneagram type because you know why they do what they do, act how they act, and want what they want.

Applying your knowledge of the Enneagram makes you a better person in society and an ambassador of understanding. An Enneagram is a fantastic tool for helping us understand who we are, and this makes us understand how to build, satisfy, and reach our full potential. The Enneagram as a tool is also used for personal growth if applied correctly. The major concern or discourse in this chapter is the way Enneagram is applied to all our activities. It explains how discovering our type of personality should be handled.

Applying knowledge of the Enneagram actually makes it easier to act and work on challenges of every personality. It should be noted that knowledge of the application on Enneagram is in different ways. We can apply it as a self-discovery tool; it can also be applied for self-enlightenment. However, when people first discover the kind of personality they possess, some of them just want to change to another personality, which indicates that they are being judgmental towards other personality types. The key to using the Enneagram is exploration without judgments.

Also, getting or seeking help and advice or coach on the application of your personality to daily life and how to enjoy being the type that you are helping to develop your character and making the world a better place. The application of your personality or Enneagram appropriately gives the ability to discover the hidden potentials within and to realize that no matter what type you are, there are possibilities of your potentials.

It should be noted that no one type is better than the other and different scholars have noted that the Enneagram can be applied to two basic aspects of human life; it can be applied to the personal or spiritual life. We can also apply the Enneagram to day to day activities of different personalities to manage and motivate people.

Now that you have this incredible knowledge, why not go ahead and be the best version of yourself? Don't be scared of applying Enneagram to your daily life. That way, you will be able to see people and things around us more clearly. Go out there and rule your world.

Chapter Nineteen
The Wings of the Enneagram Personalities

Everyone falls into the category of one of the nine basic personality types. However, we are also a bit of one of the two types that are adjacent to that basic type on either side in the circumstance of the Enneagram. This is called a wing. Although dominated by their primary personality type, people have a personality type that compliments the primary type. In order to achieve a complete understanding of one's personality or that of others, the wing must be taken into consideration.

A person of the first personality would either have a nine-wing or two-wing. A full understanding of a person's personality comes from the proper mixing of the dominant personality type and any one of its wings. Although it has been said that a person exhibits one out of the two wings, it's been found out that some people show both wings while some have such a dominating primary type that they exhibit very little of either wing.

In a strict sense, every personality actually does have two wings making it possible for both to be operative in an individual with the personality. Meanwhile, the basic personality can be so dominating that it leaves very little room for the wings — the blend of the basic type and the wing births a new name for the mixed personality.

The wings of each personality type are

Personality One (The Reformer) has Nine-wing and Two-wing

The Reformer with a Nine-wing is called The Idealist: This wing gives Reformers the aura of Peacemaker (personality nine) when they are the dominant wing although sometimes, they fail at curbing their anger. For people of personality one with this wing, the rules come first, and they are less open to humanity.

The Reformer with Two-wing is called The Advocate: When Reformers possess this wing rather than a nine wing, they are more open to human and interpersonal relationships which makes them more prone to jealousy.

Personality Two (The Helper) has One-wing and Three-wing

The Helper with One-wing is called the Servant: A one-wing makes a Helper (personality two) more conscious and emotional. They are very concerned about serving others; hence, the name 'Servant'. Compared to Helpers with a three-wing, they become more melancholy.

The Helper with Three-wing is called The Host/Hostess: With a Three-wing, people of personality two are more social and capable of affecting/influencing society. They are charming, which draws people to them and perform well in group activities that benefit people.

Personality Three (The Achiever) has Two-wing and Four-wing

The Achiever with Two-wing is called The Charmer: The two-wing gives people of personality three certain leadership qualities and a feeling of importance. They enjoy validation from others, and so, they like to get things done mostly for the benefit of those that they seek validation from.

The Achiever with Four-wing is called The Professional: A four-wing causes Achievers to be introverted. Rather than be compared to others, they measure the growth of their own abilities and the impact it has on society. They are easily motivated to work on things that they believe bring betterment to themselves.

Personality Four (The Individualist) has Three-wing and Five-wing

The Individualist with Three-wing is called The Aristocrat: People of personality four with a three-wing are sometimes mistaken as people of personality seven. They are outgoing and like to know they are doing the most when it comes to affecting the world. They are therefore intuitive and inventive; that is why they are mistaken for people of personality seven.

Personality Five (The Investigator) has Four-wing and Six-wing

The Investigator with Four-wing is called The Iconoclast: With the four-wing, people of personality five can possess a sort of artistic talent. They enjoy the aesthetics of thought, and so sometimes they can seem so withdrawn and absent-minded. Other times, they are very bubbly.

The Investigator with Six-wing is called The Problem Solver: This wing makes people of personality five very intellectual people, and they pay a lot of attention to details. They analyze situations well, making it easy for them to find answers, giving them the name 'Problem Solver'.

Personality Six (The Loyalist) has Five-wing and Seven-wing

The Loyalist with Five-wing is called The Defender: People of personality six with this wing find interests in a lot of fields and are somehow skillful in those fields. They are very doubtful and are always testing people, but once they achieve that level of trust, they make very long-lasting relationships.

The Loyalist with Seven-Wing is called The Buddy: Most of the time, all these people want is to find acceptance, and with their extroverted nature, they go after people to achieve those friendships. They are sometimes contradicting but they receive people warmly.

Personality Seven (The Enthusiast) has Six-wing and Right-wing
The Challenger with Seven-wing is called The Maverick: The challenger with a seven-wing possesses powers and are always willing to broaden their horizons. They are extroverted and always go for whatever they desire no matter the lengths they have to go to including manipulating and using other people.

Personality Eight (The Challenger) has Seven-wing and Nine-wing

The Challenger with Nine-wing is called The Bear: The confidence mixed with the calmness of people of this personality right with a nine-wing makes them authoritative like royalty or natural born leaders. They are domineering but very calm about it. They manifest by their ability to hold back anger, but when they do let it out, it can come in the form of an explosion.

<u>Personality Nine (The Peacemaker) has Eight-wing and One-wing</u>

The Peacemaker with One-wing is called The Dreamer: Dreamers mostly do everything to please. They try their best to avoid hurting anybody in any way. They are often very composed but sometimes; a spontaneous side escapes from them. They always strive to be a good person in all situations else. They remove themselves.

Chapter Twenty
The Neuroscience of Enneagram

Human intelligence is indicated in the three ways on the level of the human mind. Different psychologists have written their own view about the basic constituents of the human mind and whole in relation to their personalities. However, the neuroscience of Enneagram entails the science behind the personality system. It also explores the fact that the nine personalities of the Enneagram are surrounded by a pattern of emotion regulation that relates to inborn human emotional systems like fright, anxiety, fury, and distress. In order to understand the way in which the human mind, systems, and functions relate, it is essential to note that the human brain relates to the human mind. This explains the relationship between the three ways on the level of the human mind from the perspective that explains rational thinking in the field of neuroscience. Like it or not, humans are just way more advanced animals.

After a lot of research, it has been found that animals, no matter how primitive also express emotion, most especially fear and anger and through evolution, the emotional systems get more sophisticated in mammals. Recently, the interest in research on emotion and its regulation has increased drastically. Although there is still a lot to learn, there has been enough information about the Enneagram. It has been derived that each Enneagram type has been built around a specific emotional regulation pattern mostly in relation to fear, anger, and panic. The patterns are said to manifest while we're still young as cognitive-emotional structures that are rooted deep in the wiring of our brains.

Since the emotional structures and habits that make us our Enneagram types are said to be rooted in the wiring of our brains, it means our reactions and behaviors are defined even if they aren't very likable. Fortunately, with these habits, we have the opportunity of learning and adapting as we grow till eventually, we learn what it's like to develop control. There is a proposition of these emotional structures concerning Fear, Rage, and Panic from the perspectives of the three triads or centers of intelligence of the Enneagram types. The personalities in the triad manifest suppress or reframe the concerned emotion.

Head Centre/Triad

Personalities five, six and seven

Remember it was said that FEAR is the main emotional issue for this triad. Neurologically speaking, these people are most likely born with a tendency of fearful temperament. While personality five chooses to hide their fear and cover up their fears, personality six sustains and manifests their fears, doubts, and are always preparing for the unexpected. Personality seven also manifests theirs, but they do it in the opposite way. They reframe it into a form of optimism by looking instead at the silver lining in the dark clouds of the scary and loud thunderstorm.

Body/Gut Centre/Triad

Personalities eight, nine and one

Anger/Rage is the emotional issue of this triad. It is not necessarily that the people of this triad are born with temperamental tendencies toward anger, but while growing up, people around them came off as annoying, pushy and disturbing hence they grow up with a lot of anger at and toward a lot of things or people. Personality 8 who are the ones known to come off as intimidating manifest their rage and use it as a tool. Personality nine, on the other hand, will change this anger to a form of more attention to the other party in a bid to make the peace they always crave. Personality one hides their rage and gives it no room to manifest.

Heart Centre/Triad

Personalities two, three, and four

Panic is the concerned emotion of this triad. Mostly, people of this triad grow up without the care and attention that they desire or need.

This gets them jumpy and always feeling needy. Personality four is constantly expressing panic and a sense of loss of connection. Personality three hides and shows their feelings of panic less and probably not at all. Personality two, therefore, changes their own into a feeling of care and deriving comfort from that.

It's been found that while positive emotions motivate us, the negative emotions teach us and aid in adaptability. The teaching on Enneagram enlightens and addresses our drives and emotions

Conclusion

I must admit it's been quite a journey since the beginning of this book and I also commend your patience so far. However, it is still important to know that as entertaining as learning about personalities are, Enneagram goes beyond pure entertainment, the goal is to make relating easier and also, to give a deeper insight of understanding to a person about his or her strengths, weaknesses, preferences and attitude toward certain things.

The way you relate with people has a whole lot to do with understanding yourself and your personality which is definitely a major focus of the Enneagram as discussed in this book. Knowledge of your personality through the Enneagram is a revelation of yourself and that revelation will go a long way in helping you live a life of bliss, harmony, and help you live in a peaceful environment.

When you take the extra step of learning about others around you, you take a step towards developing and embracing a better relationship with everyone around you. It is no mystery that, when a cordial relationship is developed, you can be rest assured that you can live without holding grudges against anyone. Now it's up to you to put all the knowledge you've gained to good use and give the universe no other choice than to reward you by giving you peace. Turn obstacles to building blocks, build relationships with ease and most importantly, know who you are. Now, go out there and make a difference.

Thank you and God Bless!

References

- Helen Palmer (1991). The Enneagram: Understanding Yourself and Others in Your Life.
- Riso, Don Richard; Hudson, Russ (2000). Understanding the Enneagram; the practical guide to personality types.
- Daniel Davids (2000). The Essential Enneagram
- Naranjo, Claudio (1994). Character and Neurosis; An Integrative View.
- Nardi, The Neuroscience of Personality: Brain Savvy Insights for All Types of People.
- Fauvre, Katherine Chernick, (1995). Enneagram Instinctual Subtypes. Enneagram Explorations.
- Riso, Don Richard; Hudson, Russ (1999). Wisdom of the Enneagram.
- Helen Palmer, The Enneagram, p.36
- Baron Renee, What Type Am I: Discover Who You Really Are.
- Goldberg, Michael J. (1999). 9 Ways of Working
- Wagele, Elizabeth; Ingrid Stabb(2010). The Career Within You.
- Gilbert, Eleonora (2015). Conversations on The Enneagram.
- Sheppard, L. 2000. The Everyday Enneagram. Nine points Press: CA
- Helen Palmer. The Enneagram and The Enneagram in Love and Work.
- Naranjo, C.1990. Ennea-type Structures
- Maslow, A.H 1954. Motivation and personality.
- Richard Riso: Personality Types

- Michael Goldberg; Insider's guide to the Nine personality types: How to use the Enneagram for success at work.
- Richard Rohr and Andreas Ebert: Discovering the Enneagram.
- https://www.enneagramworldwide.com/instinctual-subtypes/
- www.Enneagram.Worldwide.com
- www.EnneagramInstitute.com
- www.internationalenneagram.org
- https://www.eclecticenergies.com/enneagram/variants
- https://www.typologycentral.com/forums/instinctual subtypes/23158-descriptions-enneagram-instinctual-variants.html
- http://personalityandthebrain.org/
- https://ninepaths.com/tag/neuroscience-of-personality/
- https://en.m.wikipedia.org/wiki/Enneagram_of_Personality.

www.ingramcontent.com/pod-product-compliance
Lightning Source LLC
Chambersburg PA
CBHW032045290426
44110CB00012B/965